ROME
and the Vatican

CENTRO STAMPA EDITORIALE

plurigraf

PERSEUS

PG-RO3 G1

Text: Loretta Santini – Cinzia Valigi

Photographs: ARCHIVIO PLURIGRAF, BIANCHI, CARFAGNA, GEROLIMETTO, MARKA, RENIS, SENZANONNA, SPERANDEI, STRADELLA, VESCOVO.

Aerial photos authorization S.M.A. 1257 del 21-12-1992.

Index

Introduction

Rome has been defined as the Eternal City, dubbed as the *Urbe*, the *caput mundi*: such names sum up perfectly the age-old and everlasting importance of this city, the cradle of western civilization, the nucleus of the political life of the then-known world and, for centuries, the centre of Christianity.

Its foundation on the banks of the Tiber is attributed to Romulus (23 April, 753 B.C., the so-called date-of-birth of Rome), who was also, as legend has it, the first of the seven kings. The expansion of the city towards its neighbouring regions got underway during the monarchic period. With the expulsion of the last monarch, Tarquinius Superbus, the Republican age began (509). In this period its political organization took shape, laws were codified and the bases laid for the future administrative structure of the state.

First under Caesar and then under Augustus, the foundations of the Empire were laid, which led to a fundamental revision of Rome's political and administrative organization. The Roman Empire, which was to last until 476 A.D., became, under its various rulers, a vast entity: it included all the countries of the Mediterranean, taking in ancient Mesopotamia to the east and pushing up to the extreme north of Europe as far as the *vallum Hadriani* (Britain) which constituted its outermost boundary.

Rome has left indelible marks of its civilization everywhere, in the form of monuments, impressive works of civil engineering. The influence of Rome's legal system is felt everywhere, providing the foundation of those laws which were to become an integral part of modern western states.

Latin, the language of the Eternal City, spread everywhere and as it met and blended with local dialects, came to constitute the common root of the various European languages.

The universal character of Rome was destined to continue and indeed to become even stronger as a result of the establishment of the Church when Rome became the Holy City. Even in the period considered to be the darkest in human history, that is in the Middle Ages, when the Empire had been divided into the Western Roman and the Eastern Roman Empire, and even later when the political strength of Rome had declined and Italy was overrun with peoples from beyond the Alps, the city continued to be the conceptual hub of the Catholic world.

The presence of the Papacy gave the Eternal City a predominant role: the Popes were both spiritual and political leaders: the central role played by the Church gave Rome a supremacy unequalled throughout the world. All this led, in each subsequent epoch, to the growth and embellishment of the city and explains the erection of the manifold splendid monuments - churches and palaces - which, in conjunction with the vestiges of the classical period, turned the Eternal City, especially in the Renaissance and Baroque period, into one of the most dazzling artistic showcases ever created.

It was, in fact, thanks to the Papacy that in the Renaissance age the city was the object of an energetic activity at the cultural and artistic level unmatched since ancient times. Such splendour found its greatest expression in the building of the new Basilica of St. Peter's and the Vatican Palaces complex with their unrivalled masterpieces by Bramante, Raphael and Michelangelo which represent the greatest artistic expression of all time.

During the Counter-Reformation (second half of the 16th century) there was a momentary lull in the building of great monuments, but the seventeenth century saw a return to the expression of the wealth and patronage of the Church and of the opulent Roman society:

palaces, churches, fountains and gardens - splendid examples of Baroque - further enriched the city. The greatest expression of Baroque art in the period was provided by the two great architects and sculptors Bernini and Borromini and, among the various painters, Caravaggio was predominant.

The following centuries, prior to the unification of Italy and the proclamation of Rome as capital, were not without important works and movements: although changing political and economic conditions meant it was no longer the sole protagonist in the artistic and cultural field, Rome, thanks to its glorious past and the range of cultural events which had distinguished it for so many centuries, remained the spiritual leader of Christianity and the conceptual point of reference for western civilization.

In conclusion, Rome offers an historical, artistic and monumental heritage of universal value, given that Roman civilization was, together with its Greek counterpart, the great cradle of western civilization. If the Greeks gave of their best in terms of literature, art, philosophy and in the life of the spirit, the Romans, with greater practical and rational sense, dedicated themselves more to politics, administration and the organization of the Empire. This difference in character is reflected in their works of art. Whereas the Greeks sought after sheer harmony and beauty, the Roman monuments are characterized by a sense of majesty and power as well as utility. This is the predominant feature of Roman architecture which will inevitably strike anyone visiting the Forums, the Amphitheatres, the Basilicas and triumphal arches.

To sum up, the city's history, its culture and its art justify the definition of Rome as the *caput mundi*, that is the capital of the world.

Its majesty, its beauty, its remarkable monumental heritage render it eternal. In addition the presence of the Pope, successor to Peter, makes it the capital of Christianity and the cultural and moral centre for Catholics everywhere.

The Piazza Venezia

Situated at the centre of Rome, the piazza is one of the most scenic in the whole city. Rectangular in shape, its focal point is the **Victor Emanuel Monument:** the huge marble «wedding-cake» raised to the first king of united Italy, Vittorio Emanuele II. The piazza is the point of confluence of the city's most important streets: the Via del Corso, the Via Quattro Novembre, the Via del Plebiscito which leads by way of the Corso Vittorio Emanuele to St. Peter's, and the Via dei Fori Imperiali, which flanks the ancient ruins of the Roman Forum and leads to the Colosseum. The piazza, thanks to its central position, is a convenient point of departure for various tourist itineraries.

THE PALAZZO VENEZIA

Built for Cardinal Pietro Barbo, later to become Pope Paul II, in 1455, the palace is attributed by some scholars to the distinguished Renaissance architect Leon Battista Alberti. Considered one of the very first buildings in the Renaissance style in the city, it is very austere in appearance and presents a brown-stuccoed façade relieved by three orders of windows in white marble; particularly striking are those in the shape of a Guelf cross on the first floor. The building now houses the interesting **Museum of the Palazzo Venezia** which contains important medieval and Renaissance works of art, and *collections of porcelain and silver* dating to various periods.
Particularly noteworthy is the Throne Room (Sala Regia) in which are displayed precious Flemish, German and Italian *tapestries* of the 15th and 16th century and a magnificent series of *arms and armour* datable from the 9th to the 16th century. The *silverware collection* is displayed in two rooms and comprises some fine examples of gold and silversmith's work, including such genuine masterpieces as the *Orsini Cross* (1334) and the **Triptych of Alba Fucense**.

Piazza Venezia: at the heart of Rome, it is the starting point of the city's main streets.

THE BASILICA OF S. MARCO

Annexed to the Palazzo Venezia is the **Basilica of San Marco,** founded in the 4th century, but completely reconstructed, after various interventions, by Cardinal Pietro Barbo in 1455-71. The façade, in elegant Renaissance style, probably designed by Giuliano Da Maiano, is adorned by a handsome portico formed of three arcades surmounted by the Loggia of the Benediction. The interior, after its restoration by F. Barigioni between 1740 and 1750, is decorated in a pure baroque style. But of the Renaissance church the beautiful wooden *coffered ceiling*, the work of Giovannino and Marco de' Dolci, survives. Some wonderful 9th century *mosaics* depicting Christ, the Apostles and some saints are preserved in the apse. Displayed in the Sacristy are a 15th century *altar* by Mino da Fiesole and a painting of the *Evangelist St. Mark* by Melozzo da Forlì. Outside the basilica, in the Piazzetta San Marco, stands one of the so-called « speaking statues of the city » - the mouthpiece of satirical pasquinades - popularly known as ***Madama Lucrezia***: the statue is thought to represent the goddess Isis.

THE VICTOR EMANUEL MONUMENT

The colossal white monument dedicated to the memory of Italy's first king, Vittorio Emanuele II, and also known as the **Vittoriano**, stands out clearly in the background of the Piazza Venezia. Designed by Giuseppe Sacconi and erected to commemorate the unification of Italy after the Risorgimento, it celebrates the great patriotic and military values which had triumphed to forge Italy into a single Nation. The monument was begun in 1885, but was not completed till forty years later. The vast central stairway leads to the **Altar of the Nation** with the **Tomb of the Unknown Soldier** which contains the remains of an unnamed soldier who died fighting for the country during the First World War; two sentinels keep constant guard over it. Above the shrine, placed within a niche, is the statue of *Roma*, flanked on either side by celebratory reliefs: to the left the *Triumphal Processions of Work*, and to the right *Patriotic Love*, sculpted by Angelo Zanelli. To the side of the ceremonial staircase are two *fountains* representing the Tyrrhenian Sea (to the right) and the Adriatic Sea (to the left). In front of the latter are the remains of the *Tomb of Publicius Bibulus*, dating to the 1st century B.C. At the centre of the monument stands the colossal ***equestrian statue of Victor Emanuel***, the work of **Enrico Chiaradia**. The stàtue is supported on a large plinth decorated with symbolic sculptures of the most important cities of Italy, the work of **Maccagnini.** Above, a wide arcaded colonnade is decorated with a series of figures representing the regions of Italy, and completed by two lateral propylaea bearing huge bronze chariots with Winged Victories at their reins. Inside, the Monument houses the **Institute for the History of the Italian Risorgimento**, the **Library** and the **Central Museum of the Risorgimento with archive annexed.**

The Victor Emanuel Monument: a spectacular and impressive building considered to be the Altar of the Nation. It contains the Tomb of the Unknown Soldier.

The Capitoline

In ancient times the focal point of religious life, the **Capitoline**, the most famous of the seven hills of Rome, constitutes the area where the most significant events in the history of the city took place. The hill consists of two summits, at the centre of which now extends the Piazza del Campidoglio, at one time the *asylum*, i.e. the area granted by Romulus to the plebs. On one of the two heights now stands the **church of Santa Maria in Aracoeli**, its site occupied in ancient times by the Capitoline Shrine. On the other stood the great **Temple of Jupiter Optimus Maximus**. From the steep cliffs of the southern part of the hill, known in ancient times as *Mons Tarpeius* - the Tarpeian Rock -, traitors of the country were thrown to their death; remains of the **Temple of Jupiter** can be seen close to it. The architectural complex of the Piazza del Campidoglio, now the centre of the public life of the city, owes its harmonious appearance to the genius of **Michelangelo,** who designed it for Pope Paul III.

THE PIAZZA DEL CAMPIDOGLIO

Conceived by the great mind of the artist, the piazza is delimited by three palaces: the two diverging palaces either side, on the right the **Palazzo dei Conservatori**, on the left the **Palazzo Nuovo** open up the space and frame the **Palazzo Senatorio** with its double staircase. The piazza is linked to the city by means of an imposing graded ramp, it too bearing the stamp of **Michelangelo**, at whose foot stand two *Egyptian lions*. At the head of the stairs are the colossal statues of the *Dioscuri*, Castor and Pollux with their horses; they are flanked, along the balustrade which runs all the way around the piazza, by the *Trophies of Marius,* the *statues of Constantine and Constantine II,* and, finally by two milestone columns brought from the Via Appia. The dynamic effect which characterises the piazza is emphasised by the design of the paving enclosed in an oval, at whose centre stands the copy of the *equestrian statue of Marcus Aurelius*, recently restored and awaiting the gold patination which originally distinguished it. The statue (the original is housed in the so-called Roman Garden), the only one of equestrian type preserved from Roman antiquity, dates back to the 2nd century A.D., and tradition has it that it has only survived because it was believed to represent Constantine, the first Christian Emperor.
The Capitoline Museums are undergoing restoration and the exhibits have been temporarily transferred to other Museums.

THE PALAZZO SENATORIO

The palace, now the Town Hall and seat of the municipal council of Rome, faces onto the piazza with an imposing façade. At its base is a double stairway, below which - at the centre of its twin ramps - is a niche containing a *statue of the Goddess Roma* who holds an orb in her hand, emblem of the rule of Rome over the world. She is flanked by two colossal *statues of river-gods* representing the Nile and the Tigris, the latter later transformed into the Tiber. The palace was built on the site of the ancient

Tabularium. Behind it rises the bell-tower, erected by Martino Longhi the Elder in the 16th century. A series of large and interesting rooms are contained inside the Palazzo Senatorio; among the most famous are the **Room of the Banners,** the **Council Hall** dominated by its *statue of Julius Caesar,* and the **Protomoteca Capitolina,** a *collection of busts* of famous men installed here in 1950.
By descending the Via del Campidoglio to the side of the Palazzo Senatorio, we can see the remains of the famous **Temple of Vejove**, an ancient Italic deity, which came to light during the work of reconstruction.

THE PALAZZO NUOVO

The building, situated to the left of the Piazza del Campidoglio, was designed by **Michelangelo** on the model of the Palazzo dei Conservatori facing it on the other side of the piazza. It was only built in the 17th century, when it was decided to enhance the piazza's perspective effect and so give it the harmoniousness and coherence that distinguish it today. The Palazzo Nuovo now houses the **Capitoline Museum,** which contains an ancient collection of works of sculpture of the classical period. In the courtyard is the *Fountain of Marforio,* another of the so-called « speaking statues » of the city. The collection, originally housed in the Palazzo dei Conservatori, was set up here around the middle of the 17th century. In the Atrium is the important *statue of Minerva* (5th century B.C.); as we continue, we come to the rooms containing some beautiful sarcophagi, such as the *Amendola sarcophagus* (2nd century), that of *Alessandro Severo* and the huge *statue of Mars.*Then follow the rooms which house the **Egyptian Collection** and the **Collection of oriental cults**. Ascending to the first floor, consisting of seven rooms, we first enter a wide **Gallery** in which several interesting exhibits are displayed, including the beautiful statue of the goddess **Athena** found in Velletri; a fine **head of the emperor Probus** and **Amor drawing a bow;** the mosaic known as the **mosaic of the Doves** executed by Sosus of Pergamon, depicting *four doves* drinking from a vase; a *sarcophagus* of a child and a *Tabula Iliaca.* There is a remarkable statue of **Venus,** a copy of an earlier work dating back to the 2nd century B.C. and of noteworthy mention are the 65 *busts* of Roman emperors which constitute one of the richest and most interesting collections, also from the iconographic point of view, of the imperial period.

Room of the Philosophers: it takes its name from a series of *portraits* of Greek and Roman thinkers, such as those representing Socrates, Cicero, Homer and Lysias.

A series of valuable sculptures is distributed over the other rooms, including a noteworthy pair of *Centaurs,* executed in the Hadrianic period, and a beautiful *Wounded Amazon,* a copy of the original by Kresilas; a statue of a *Laughing Faun holding a bunch of grapes to his mouth;* the magnificent statue of an unknown warrior known as the *Dying Gaul,* found in the Orti Sallustiani.

Finally a valuable piece from the Hellenistic era depicting Eros and Psyche. Furthermore, there are numerous Roman inscriptions, among which, worthy of mention, is the bronze tablet which sets out the law of the Vespasian empire which sanctioned the powers of the emperor.

Left-hand page: *Piazza del Campidoglio - Marcus Aurelius.*

This page: *the Dying Gaul: roman copy of an original Greek statue of the 3rd century B.C.*

THE PALAZZO DEI CONSERVATORI

The palace, rebuilt by Giacomo Della Porta in the 16th century based on Michelangelo's design, contains the **Halls of the Conservators,** the **Museum of the Palazzo dei Conservatori,** the **Braccio Nuovo,** the **Museo Nuovo** and the **Capitoline Picture Gallery.** The courtyard contains the ***head of Constantine,*** recovered from the Basilica of Constantine, as well as some interesting reliefs.

In the inner rooms various works of art are housed including a fresco depicting the *Battles between Horatii and Curatii* executed by the Cavalier d'Arpino (and kept in the room of the same name), the statues of *Urban VIII* by Bernini, and *Innocent X* by A. Algardi; the beautiful sculpture known as the ***Spinario,*** made of bronze and dating back to the 1st century B.C., and above all, the famous ***Capitoline Wolf,*** a bronze group from the 5th century B.C., since time immemorial, the symbol of Rome. The twins were added by A. Pollaiolo in the 15th century.

In addition to the above-mentioned works, the palace contains numerous sculptures, friezes and valuable 18th century tapestries.

Above: *the Spinario, a bronze statue of the 1st century B.C.*
Below: *Palazzo dei Conservatori - room of the Horatii and Curatii.*

THE MUSEUM OF THE PALAZZO DEI CONSERVATORI

Especially noteworthy among its important collections of Greek and Etruscan vases and numerous sarcophagi are: the *statue of the Esquiline Venus,* a *funerary bed* with a finely decorated head, the statue of *Artemis,* that depicting a *Seated girl* dating back to the Hellensitic era, portraits of Magistrates and several heads and busts including, of particular quality, those of *Leo* and of the *Centaur.*

The **BRACCIO NUOVO** and the **MUSEO NUOVO** have been closed and are awaiting the commencement of renovation works. The former was set up in 1950-52 to house archaeological material found in the Temple of Jupiter Capitolinus, including the *statue of Apollo as an archer* from the 5th century B.C. The latter was set up in 1925 and contains Roman and Greek remains, among which the outstanding *Aphrodite* by Praxiteles.

THE CAPITOLINE PICTURE GALLERY

One thing we should on no account miss during our visit to the Campidoglio is the Capitoline Picture Gallery **(Pinacoteca Capitolina),** which contains important paintings from the Sacchetti and Pio collections.
Founded by Pope Benedict XIV in 1784, it includes famous paintings by **Rubens** (*Romulus and Remus suckled by the Wolf*), **Diego Velazquez** (*Portrait of G. Lorenzo Bernini*), **Caravaggio** (*St. John the Baptist*), as well as works by other artists of the 16th, 17th and 18th centuries. A distinguished collection of 18th century porcelain is on display in the Cini Gallery.

Above: *the Capitoline Wolf, an Etruscan bronze of the 5th century B.C., which has become the symbol of Rome.* Below: *the Capitoline Venus, copy of a statue of the 2nd century B.C.*

Above: *Palazzo Nuovo - exhibition room.*
Below: *the Capitoline Picture Gallery: "St. John the Baptist" by Caravaggio and the "Rape of the Sabine Women" by Pietro Da Cortona.*

The Church of Santa Maria in Aracoeli

Occupying the summit of the Capitoline Arx (or Acropolis), it is approached by a long votive stairway built by the population in 1348 to thank the Virgin Mary for averting the threat of the plague.

According to tradition, the church stands on the site where Augustus saw the apparition of a woman with a child who said, pointing to the altar where she was sitting: «Ecce ara primogeniti Dei»: a prophecy of the coming of Our Lord. Officiated by the Franciscan Friars Minor since 1250, the church boasts very ancient origins; in fact it was erected over the ruins of the Temple of Juno Moneta. In the 10th century it assumed the name of Santa Maria in Capitolio, which it retained till the 13th century.

The unadorned brick façade has three portals, of which the two lateral ones are adorned with lunettes bearing 16th century reliefs. The interior, consisting of a nave and two aisles divided by 22 *antique marble columns*, is notable for its fine medieval *Cosmatesque pavement* and sumptuous 16th century *coffered ceiling*, celebrating the victory over the Turks at the naval battle of Lepanto.

The many funerary monuments contained in the church include the *monument to Cardinal Ludovico d'Albret* sculpted by Andrea Bregno in 1465, and a *tomb slab* sculpted by **Donatello**. The **first chapel** to the right, dedicated to St. Bernardine, is decorated with wonderful *frescoes* by **Pinturicchio** depicting the saint. Between the nave and the transepts are two fine *pulpits* sculpted by Lorenzo and Giacomo Cosma in the 13th century. In the right transept is the *tomb of Luca Savelli* (reusing a Roman sarcophagus). The baroque high altar is adorned with a beautiful *painting of the Virgin Mary*. In the left transept is the *monument to Cardinal Matteo d'Acquasparta*, probably a work by Giovanni di Cosma. In the Sacristy is housed the venerated wooden statue of the Infant Jesus known as the **Bambino dell'Aracoeli**, before which, during the Christmas period, prayers and religious songs are recited by children from far and wide.

Church of Santa Maria in Aracoeli: it stands on the Capitoline citadel and is approached by a long flight of steps.

The Roman Forum

In ancient times the Forum was a civic piazza surrounded by basilicas, temples and monuments where the public life of the city took place. The area on which it arose was originally insalubrious and prone to flooding, but was reclaimed by various attempts at drainage over the years. The first of these was made by king Tarquinius Priscus with the construction of the **Cloaca Massima.** The place became, thanks to its position, a favourite meeting-point between the inhabitants of the city and those from the surrounding hills who saw in it an ideal market-place for selling their wares. Around this trading activity, a series of shops, temples and basilicas progressively arose, eventually transforming the area into the heart of the city, the focal point round which not only the business transactions but more especially the public life of the Roman citizen revolved. It was here that the assemblies of the people and the Senate, the elections of magistrates, the great religious ceremonies and the administration of justice took place. The enormous economic and political expansion of the city meant that the Roman Forum itself became inadequate to cope with its needs and determined the construction of others (the Imperial Forums: see below).

In 283 A.D. what had progressively grown into a monumental complex was devastated by fire; the restoration set in hand by Diocletian did not, however, mark the end of its decline or arrest its decay which continued irresistibly through the Middle Ages, hastened both by the barbarian invasions and the continuous spoliation of its materials for use in the construction of private houses and fortified strongholds. Eventually it was reduced to a pasture for cattle. Only in the 18th century did interest revive in this wonderful complex, testified by excavations and the archaeological exploration that is still continuing to this day.

The Roman Forum can be entered from the Via dei Fori Imperiali, which starts out from the Piazza Venezia to the left of the Victor Emanuel Monument. Or we can approach it by descending from the Capitoline Hill down the Clivus Capitolinus and then taking the Via del Foro Romano.

This second itinerary enables us to visit the complex consisting of the Porticus of the Dii Consentes, the Temple of Vespasian, the Temple of Concord and the Mamertine Prison.

The first monument we notice, to the

View of the Roman Forum: in the foreground the columns of the Temple of Vespasian.
Right-hand page: *panoramic view of the Forum.*
Pages 18-19: *a plastic model of the ancient Rome by I. Gismondi - Kept in the Museum of the Roman Civilization.*

left of the Clivus Capitolinus, immediately below the Tabularium, is the **Porticus of the Dii Consentes,** where *12 statues* representing the main deities of Rome were placed. Only the remains of some columns survive of the Porticus.

Close to it is the **Temple of Vespasian** erected by Domitian in 81 A.D. It is testified by the presence of three wonderful *marble columns* in the Corinthian style.

Adjacent to it, on the Via del Foro Romano, is the **Temple of Concord,** so called because it celebrated the end of hostilities between patricians and plebeians. Built in 367 B.C., it was reconstructed by Tiberius; but only a few ruins of it remain today.

Close to it stands the **church of San Giuseppe dei Falegnami,** the church of the guild of carpenters built in 1598. Below it is the famous **Mamertine Prison,** which consists of two superimposed dungeons: the Carcer Mamertinus (2nd century B.C.) and the Carcer Tullianum (3rd century B.C.). It was a place of imprisonment and death for many historical personages, such as the Gaulish king Vercingetorix and the king of Numidia, Jugurtha, the one put to death by Julius Caesar, the other starved to death by Marius. According to the legend, another prisoner incarcerated here was St. Peter, who worked a miracle by making a fountain of water spring from the floor, so that he might have water to baptize his gaolers after having converted them to Christianity. It is from this legend that the name San Pietro in Carcere, by which the building is also called, derives.

Facing it, on the other side of the road, is the **church of Santi Luca e Martina,** consisting of two superimposed churches; the lower one was founded in honour of St. Martin in the 6th century; the upper one dates to the 17th century. The handsome *travertine façade* is by Pietro da Cortona.

We now approach the main entrance to the Roman Forum, which is located on the Via dei Fori Imperiali. To the

Above: *the Mamertine Prison, where tradition has it Saint Peter was incarcerated.*
Below: *Forum: the three columns of the Temple of Castor and Pollux.*

right of the **Via Sacra,** the road which connected the various parts of the Forum and of which the original Roman paving is still visible, we see the remains of the **Basilica Aemilia.** The first basilica on the site was founded by M. Fulvius Nobilior and M. Aemilius Lepidus in 179 B.C., and was later reconstructed and enriched by other members of the gens Aemilia. The term basilica in ancient Rome denoted a large rectangular building in whose interior two or four rows of columns delimited a central nave and side aisles (a similar kind of plan was later adopted for the construction of Christian basilicas). Originally secular in purpose, it was assigned to business transactions and the administration of justice.

Adjacent to the Basilica Aemilia is the **Curia** or Senate House. Originally built as an assembly hall by Tullus Hostilius, it was reconstructed under Diocletian, and later, in the 7th century, converted into a church. Inside, the marble floor has been restored, and the marble podia on which the wooden benches of the Senators were placed are visible.

Almost in front of the Curia we may see the *Plutei of Trajan,* the marble parapets or screens which decorated the tribune of the Rostra. They are sculpted with scenes celebrating some important enterprises of Trajan's government - such as the provision made by the Emperor for the children of poor citizens - and reliefs of the principal sacrificial animals. The square in front of the Curia was in fact the **Comitium:** the place where the people gathered in assemblies to elect the magistrates and to decide on the major questions of political life.

On the edge of the Comitium, in front of the Curia, below a large paved area in black marble (*Lapis Niger*), is an underground shaft believed to be the **Tomb of Romulus;** an inscription of the 6th century B.C., the oldest so far found in the city, was preserved in it.

The magnificent triumphal arch just beyond it is the **Arch of Septimius Severus.** It was dedicated by the People and the Senate to the emperor Septimius Severus and his sons Caracalla and Geta in 203 to celebrate their victories over the Parthians, the Arabs and the Assyrians. Consisting of a central arch and two side arches, it is well-preserved and decorated with reliefs representing episodes from the wars conducted by Severus. Close to it is the **Umbilicus Urbis**, a circular base which indicated the centre of the city.

To the left of the arch we may note a tufa wall: it is all that remains of the original platform that served as the orators' tribune. The structure is called the **Rostra** because it was adorned with the bronze beaks (*rostra*) stripped from enemy ships conquered in battle.

In front of it is a small piazza (Piazza del Foro) in which stands the **Column of Phocas** (608), the last to be erected in honour of an eastern Emperor.

To the right of the Piazza del Foro we can see the remains of the **Basilica Julia,** built by Julius Caesar. Adjacent

Arch of Septimius Severus.

Following page: Partial view of the Roman Forum.

to it are the imposing remains of the **Temple of Saturn,** built in c. 500 B.C., and reconstructed in 42 B.C. The statue of the god Saturn - ancient god of the Capitol - was venerated inside it. It also served as the State Treasury. The eight columns with Ionic capitals that remain are those of the pronaos.

By taking the Via Sacra right to the end of the Piazza del Foro we come to the few remains of the **Temple of Julius Caesar,** erected on the site where the body of Caesar was cremated and where Mark Anthony read out his famous testament.

Close to it is the basement of the **Arch of Augustus,** and to its right we can see three wonderful fluted columns of the Corinthian order which formed part of the **Temple of Castor and Pollux.** It was built in honour of the Dioscuri who, according to the legend, helped the Romans in their victory over the Latins and the Tarquins at the battle of Lake Regillus.

In its immediate vicinity is the **Lacus Juturnae** where Castor and Pollux watered their horses when they brought the news of the victory to the Romans.

Behind is the **Oratory of the Forty Martyrs** and, to its left, **Santa Maria Antiqua,** the oldest Christian building of the Forum. It was built over a building of the imperial period, reconstructed and dedicated to Christian worship in the 6th century. Of considerable artistic interest are the *frescoes* that adorn its walls. Returning to the Arch of Augustus, we can see the remains of the **Regia:** seat of the Pontifex Maximus and of the archive of the annals compiled of the salient events in Roman public life. According to tradition, it occupies the site of the house of Numa Pompilius, second king of Rome.

In front of the Regia stood the **Temple of Vesta,** which can be recognised by its circular basement. It was in this temple that the sacred fire, symbolizing the life of Rome, was preserved. Guarded by the Vestals, priestesses of the goddess. Vesta, the fire was constantly kept alight, for it was consid-

Above: *the Temple of Castor and Pollux.*
Below: *the Temple of Antoninus and Faustina.*

ered a bad omen for the destiny of the city if it should ever go out. Adjacent to the circular temple was the **House of the Vestals,** the sanctuary in which the young priestesses, guardians of the sacred fire, dwelt.

Facing the Regia on the other side of the Via Sacra is the **Temple of Antoninus and Faustina,** erected in 141 A.D. in honour of the wife of Antoninus Pius and, on the latter's death, of the emperor himself: husband and wife are commemorated in the surviving inscription on the architrave. In the 11th century the temple was converted into the **church of San Lorenzo in Miranda.**

To the right of the temple is the site of an **archaic cemetery,** with burials dating to the Early Iron Age.

This is followed, on the Via Sacra, by the **Temple of Romulus,** circular in plan and dedicated to the deified son of Maxentius.

At the end of the Via Sacra is the **Arch of Titus,** consisting of a single archway. It was erected by Domitian to commemorate the victories of Vespasian and his son Titus over the Jews and the destruction of Jerusalem.

Beyond Santa Francesca Romana extends the huge double **Temple of Venus and Rome,** designed and built by the emperor Hadrian in 135. It was later (307) restored by Maxentius. The temple consisted of two apses: one (dedicated to the goddess Roma) facing towards the Forum, the other (dedicated to Venus) towards the Colosseum.

Views of the Roman Forum and the mighty vaults of the Basilica of Maxentius.

The Palatine

The Palatine is the hill on which the original nucleus of the city of Rome arose: the settlement (known as «Roma quadrata») founded by Romulus, according to legend, in 754 or 753 B.C. The hill originally had two summits: the Palatium and the Germalus (subsequently levelled by Domitian). Of the seven hills of Rome it is undoubtedly the richest and most evocative in historical remains. In the Republican period, many famous personalities of the time, including Cicero, built their houses on this hill. It became the site of numerous temples and, in the imperial period, also of the palaces of the emperors. The first of these latter was that of Tiberius: the domus Tiberiana. After the decline and fall of the Roman Empire, the architectural history of the Palatine continued in the 11th century, with the building of churches, castles and convents over the ruins of antiquity, and then in the 16th when the Farnese built the sumptuous Villa Farnese and its elaborate gardens, the Orti Farnesiani, on the hill. This noble family also deserves merit for bringing the Palatine's ancient ruins to light, even though the proper archaeological exploration of the hill had to await the more systematic excavations by Rosa, Vaglieri and Boni in the 19th century. We ascend the Palatine from the Roman Forum, by way of the Clivus Capitolinus, which we join just after the Arch of Titus. We then come to the imposing 16th century **Portal** designed by Vignola, which precedes the wonderful gardens of the **Orti Farnesiani** in which the **Farnese Pavilion,** part of their splendid villa, stands. This delightful setting is made particularly evocative by the presence of the ancient ruins we pass during our exploration of the hill. Of the **Domus Tiberiana,** the palace of the emperor Tiberius, little remains to be seen above ground, though it was supported by a huge artificial terrace. Of the **Temple of Magna Mater** or **of Cybele,** whose statue now stands in the Domus Tiberiana, the podium remains. Close to it are the remains of the **Scalae Caci**, a stairway giving access to the Palatine and of very ancient origin, and some remains of prehistoric huts: according to legend, they mark the site of the **House of Romulus.** Also extant are two circular cisterns dating to the 5th century B.C., and some remains which are attributed by tradition to Rome's first circuit of walls. From the Temple of Magna Mater we make our way down to the **House of Livia:** it was in fact the house of Augustus (Livia was his wife). Its structure and the marvellous *mural paintings* that decorated its rooms have been preserved almost intact. Close to it is an underground passageway that connected the imperial palaces: the **Cryptoporticus of Nero.** Beyond it are the impressive ruins of the **Domus Flavia,** the large and elaborate palace built by the Flavian emperors, notably Domitian. Various parts of the complex are well-preserved: the basilica, the Aula Regia or throne-room and the emperor's dining-room: the imperial **Triclinium.** A convent was built over the ruins of another adjacent palace, the **Domus Augustana:** it now houses the Antiquarium of the Palatine, a museum comprising a collection of *artefacts, sculptures* and remains of *mural paintings* found on the hill. Other ruins on the Palatine include the large **Hippodrome** or Stadium built by Domitian; the large and impressive remains of the **Domus Severiana,** part of the palace built by Septimius Severus; and the **Paedagogium**, a college for imperial pages also dating to the period of Domitian.

Left-hand page:
Arch of Titus.

View of the Palatine, the hill on which the original nucleus of Rome arose.

Views of the Palatine.

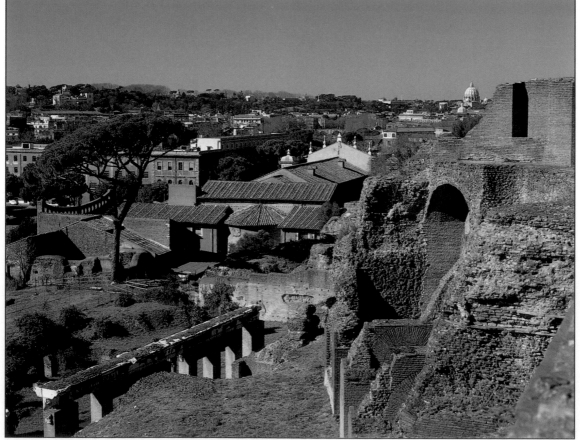

Following page: *aerial view of the area of the Palatine and its magnificent ruins.*

The Imperial Forums

The enormous political and economic expansion of Rome, and the consequent growth in judicial activity, meant that a single Forum was inadequate to cope with the increasing demands placed upon it (the Roman Forum, in any case, could not be enlarged due to the lack of building space). It was Caesar who first built another one, towards the end of the Republic: this was the Forum Julium, laid out in the environs of the Campus Martius. This was followed by the successive addition of the Forum of Augustus, the Forum of Vespasian, the Forum of Nerva and the Forum of Trajan. Our visit to the Imperial Forums has the Piazza Venezia as its departure point. Turning into the Via dei Fori Imperiali to the left of the Victor Emanuel Monument, we immediately come to the Piazza del Foro Traiano, on which two adjacent churches stand: the Renaissance **church of Santa Maria di Loreto** and the 18th century **church of the Holy Name of Mary.** Facing them are the wonderful remains of the **Forum of Trajan,** designed by Apollodorus of Damascus and built between 107 and 113: it was thus the last of the Imperial Forums to be built. Grandiose in conception, it was laid out round a central square, which was flanked by two lateral arcades; the complex of the **Basilica Ulpia** and the **Libraries;** and, on the opposite side, the **Temple of Trajan.** At the centre of the square stood an equestrian statue of the emperor. To one side of the Basilica Ulpia we can still admire **Trajan's Column,** dedicated to M. Ulpius Traianus and commemorating his victorious expeditions against the Dacians (it is 40 m high excluding the basement). Tommaso della Porta's bronze *statue of St. Peter* has stood on top of the column since 1587. The shaft of the column, consisting of 18 superimposed blocks of marble, is decorated with a continuous spiral

A view of the Imperial Forums and, in the photo above, a detail of Trajan's Column.

frieze immortalizing, in wonderful reliefs, the emperor's victorious campaigns in Dacia. The basement of the column houses the sepulchral chamber in which the emperor wished his ashes to be preserved. Adjacent to the column are the much-depleted ruins of the **Basilica Ulpia**, but the remains of the columns attest to the grandeur of its architectural plan, consisting of five aisles. To the rear of the Forum of Trajan is the imposing hemicycle of the **Markets of Trajan**, a commercial complex consisting of three levels of shops; a large hall was also used as a market. Continuing along the Via dei Fori Imperiali, we now come to the **Forum of Augustus**. It was erected to commemorate the victorious battle of Philippi, fought by Augustus in 42 A.D.: the battle in which Brutus and Cassius, the assassins of Caesar, met their death. Of the **Temple of Mars Ultor** (the god of war to whom the whole Forum was dedicated) some magnificent fluted columns and the frontal stairway remain. Also identifiable are the meagre ruins of the two basilicas and a few other architectural features which formed part of the Forum. Next to the Forum of Augustus is the **Forum of Nerva** (97 A.D.), also called the Forum Transitorium because it provided transit between the popular district of the Suburra, the Roman Forum and the other Forums. Within it stood the Temple of Minerva, whose basement podium remains at the centre of the Forum. Other remains, at its further end, consist of two half-buried Corinthian columns (known as the Colonnacce). There follows the **Forum of Peace** or **Forum of Vespasian,** of which little remains other than an exedra and some prostrate fragments of column (in front). The **church of Saints Cosmas and Damian** was built over the ruins of a hall forming part of the Forum. On the other side of the Via dei Fori Imperiali, immediately after the Victor Emanuel Monument, is the **Forum of Caesar,** in front of which stands an imposing bronze *statue of Julius Caesar*. At the centre of the large piazza of the Forum the emperor erected the **Temple of Venus Genitrix,** whom the Julian clan claimed as ancestress. Other remains form part of the **Basilica Argentaria.**

Above: *the Trajan Markets complex.* Below: *Forum of Augustus - podium of the Temple of Mars.*

The Colosseum

This is the term commonly used to indicate the Flavian Amphitheatre; it perhaps derives from the fact that a gigantic statue of Nero known as the Colossus was situated adjacent to it. Begun by Vespasian in 72, the Colosseum was completed by his son Titus in the year 80: Titus set aside 100 days of festivity to celebrate its inauguration. It could contain up to 50,000 spectators, who gathered there to watch the famous games which were often cruel, but which aroused enormous enthusiasm in the spectators. The shows staged in the Colosseum included contests between gladiators (in general, specially trained slaves), the hunting of and battles between wild animals (brought to Rome from the farthest outposts of the Empire), and naval engagement or *naumachie* (mock sea-fights), to simulate which the arena was flooded with water. The Colosseum was also the place of martyrdom of many early Christians. It goes without saying that, in the building of the Colosseum, the Romans gave proof of all their technical skills and incredible inventiveness. For instance, a system was devised to protect the spectators both from the rain and the heat by a system of awnings overhead (the «Velarium»), the fixtures to support which are still visible in the upper walls. The Amphitheatre, literally a «double theatre», was so called because it derives from the fusion of two theatres which in ancient Greece consisted of a semicircular series of tiered seats rising from a central orchestra and stage. The result was the creation of an enormous elliptical ring of marble-veneered travertine, rising in four storeys, of which the first three presented arcades with half-columns respectively of the Doric, Ionic and Corinthian orders between them. The top storey, more compact and decorated with Corinthian pilaster strips, was pierced by windows. What we see of the Colosseum today is what remains of this mighty edifice after the depredations of nature (it has been damaged by various earthquakes) and of man, who has not hesitated to use it as a quarry for building materials, and to strip it of marbles and other precious decorations.

The speedy entry and exit of spectators was ensured by the placing of the eighty entrances right round the ground-floor arcades, each of them numbered to indicate the staircases leading to the various sectors of the tiered seating, each of them reserved for a particular category or class: the first for the emperor and the Vestals, and so on right up to the topmost gallery where the common people and women sat. The arena, whose floor has been removed, reveals a complex underground system, which included the various mechanisms and apparatus for the games, and the corridors for the transit of the gladiators and the wild beasts. The site of the Colossus of Nero, at the end of the Via dei Fori Imperiali, is marked by some travertine slabs set into the road; the gilt bronze statue is thought to have been some 30 m. high.

Near to it is the **Arch of Constantine,** a magnificent triple-arcaded triumphal arch raised by the people and the Senate in 312 to celebrate Constantine's victory over Maxentius in the battle of the Milvian Bridge. Composite in its decoration, the arch incorporates medallions and reliefs spoliated from earlier imperial monuments. Its state of conservation is excellent. In front of the Arch of Constantine was the ***Meta Sudans***, a conical brick fountain built by Titus at the end of the 1st century A.D. According to tradition, the gladiators washed and quenched their thirst at this fountain after their contests in the Colosseum. Only the foundations now remain.

Behind the Colosseum rises the **Oppian**, one of the three heights of the Esquiline, another of the seven hills of Rome. A park now extends over it, incorporating various Roman ruins, including the remains of the **Domus Aurea.** This sumptuously decorated building was the palace of the emperor Nero. On his death, it was covered over by the subsequent construction of the **Baths of Trajan**. Underground, it is still possible to admire its long corridors and splendidly frescoed rooms: a truly atmospheric sight which was a source of inspiration to many Renaissance artists.

Previous pages:
the Colosseum.

This page:
*the magnificent
Arch of
Constantine.*

The Theatre of Marcellus

Let us now walk along the Via del Teatro Marcello. Turning immediately to the right we come to the Piazza Campitelli on which stands the **church of Santa Maria in Campitelli,** built by Rainaldi in the 17th century, a distinctive example of the late Roman Baroque style. Inside is housed an enamelled icon of the *Madonna in Portico* dating to the 11th century, in honour of whom the church was built to mark the end of the plague epidemic of 1656. Close by, in the Via dei Funari, is the **church of Santa Caterina dei Funari,** dating back to the 12th century. Reconstructed during the 16th century, it has a splendid façade by G. Guidetti, it too dating to the 16th century. On the same street is the **Palazzo Mattei di Giove,** built by Maderno towards the end of the 16th century. At its end is the Piazza Mattei, dominated by its charming Renaissance **Fountain of the Tortoises**. Designed by Giacomo Della Porta, the fountain consists of bronze ephebes supporting tortoises, though these were added in the 17th century; the bronze figures are by Taddeo Landini. We return to the Via del Teatro Marcello. A short distance ahead, to the right, is the **Theatre of Marcellus.** It was actually built by Augustus in the 1st century B.C. in honour of his young nephew Marcellus, whom he intended as his successor but who was cut off by an early death. The Theatre is partly occupied by the **Palazzo Orsini,** but some of the two series of superimposed tiers of arches that composed it are still visible. Adjacent to it stand three graceful Corinthian columns: all that remains of the **Temple of Apollo Sosiano** erected in 433-31 B.C. The Theatre abuts onto the Piazza di Monte Savello, on which also stands the **church of San Nicola in Carcere,** built over the ruins of three temples, as is clearly attested by the remains of ancient columns incorporated into its walls. The 16th century *façade* is by Della Porta who made various alterations to the original building dating to the 11th century.

The stretch of the Tiber facing the piazza on which the church stands is that in which the **Isola Tiberina** lies, the island

Above: *the Theatre of Marcellus.*
Below: *the Fountain of the Tortoises.*

Above: *aerial view of the Isola Tiberina.*

Below: *the Synagogue.*

sacred in ancient times to the god of medicine Aesculapius, to whom a temple was dedicated. The island's medical associations live on in the **Hospital of the Fatebenefratelli** which is now situated on it (founded in the 16th century). Adjacent to it is the **church of San Giovanni Calibita** of the 17th century, while on the other side of the little piazza is the **church of San Bartolomeo** built by the emperor Otto III over the ruins of the Temple of Aesculapius.

We cross the Pons Fabricius; nearby is the **Portico of Octavia,** built in 146 B.C. and reconstructed by Augustus in honour of his sister. Only some columns, part of the entablature and an arch survive of it: they form an entrance to the **church of Sant'Angelo in Peschiera,** which derives its name from the fish-market once situated here. The whole surrounding area is the characteristic Jewish quarter in Rome: the **Ghetto.** We now return to the Theatre of Marcellus. Continuing our way along the Via del Teatro Marcello, we pass the medieval **House of the Crescenzi,** incorporating Roman reliefs and other ancient architectural fragments in its structure, and so come to the Piazza della Bocca della Verità. It marks the site of the

ancient Forum Boarium. The remains of two ancient temples still stand in the piazza. The rectangular one is the so-called **Temple of Fortuna Virilis,** dating to the 2nd century B.C., and built in an Italo-Greek style which represents a fusion of Hellenistic and Etruscan features. Adjacent to it is the graceful **Temple of Vesta.** In structure and circular plan it is of Greek derivation; but the Romans saw in this a reflection of the form of the primitive huts familiar to them. The temple consists of a circular peristyle of Corinthian columns which originally supported an entablature of which no trace remains. It was not in fact dedicated to Vesta: only its circular plan inspired this name. On the other side of the piazza stands the **church of Santa Maria in Cosmedin,** erected over the remains of Roman buildings in the 6th century and subsequently enlarged and transformed. Its tall and beautiful belltower pierced by two- and three-light mullioned windows is in the Romanesque style (12th century). In the portico of the church is preserved a large circular stone mask: this is the famous «**Bocca della Verità**» (mouth of truth) from which the piazza takes its name. The name derives from the legend that if a witness whose truthfulness was doubted placed his hand in the mouth of the mask, it would bite him if he were guilty of telling a lie. Not far away, at the centre of the Via del Velabro, is the **Arch of Janus,** dating to the period of the emperor Constantine. It has four equal sides, with arches opening to the four points of the compass. Close to it stands the **church of San Giorgio in Velabro,** dating to the 6th century but subjected to various alterations since then. It is flanked by a graceful Romanesque bell-tower (12th century). The interior is in basilica form. The apse is decorated with *frescoes* dating to 1295, perhaps the work of Pietro Cavallini. Of considerable artistic interest is also the *Cosmatesque baldacchino.* Adjacent to the church is the **Arcus Argentarius,** raised in 204 and dedicated to the emperor Septimius Severus, his wife Julia Domna and his sons Caracalla and Geta. Close to the arch is the drainage channel of the **Cloaca Maxima,** which debouches into the Tiber at this point. This daring work

Above: *the Church of Santa Maria in Cosmedin.*
Below: *the Bocca della Verità, the famous stone mask.*

of hydraulic engineering, perhaps dating back to the period of Tarquinius Priscus, was used to drain the once marshy ground of the Forum. We now make our way towards the Circus Maximus, which still preserves the shape of ancient Rome's chariot-racing track, and, by way of the Via del Circo Massimo, ascend the **Aventine,** another of the hills of Rome, its slopes dotted with secluded villas and laid out with little parks and gardens. Some ancient remains are also to be seen on the hill: a stretch of the Republican walls of Rome and some buildings dating to the time of Augustus. The Piazzale Romolo e Remo is dominated by a monument to Giuseppe Mazzini (1949). On ascending the Aventine, we come to the **church of Santa Sabina,** on the Piazza d'Illiria. Dating back to the 5th century, it still retains, in spite of the numerous alterations to which it has been subject over the centuries, the most characteristic features of an Early Christian basilica. A large 5th century *mosaic* is preserved above the main portal. The interior is divided into a nave and two aisles by 24 fluted Corinthian columns. On the same road we come to the **church of Santi Bonifacio e Alessio,** (founded in the 10th century), but reconstructed by T. De Marchis in the 18th century. In the Piazza dei Cavalieri di Malta is the **Villa of the Priorate of Malta** and the **church of Santa Maria del Priorato.** After passing the Piazza Sant'Anselmo, we now descend the street of the same name and so reach the Piazza Albania. Close to the piazza is the **church of San Saba** (7th century) with a Romanesque façade. We now continue down to the nearby **Porta San Paolo,** in ancient times known as the Porta Ostiensis, which leads to the basilica of St. Paul Outside the Walls. To the right is the **Pyramid of Caius Cestius** from the end of the 1st century B.C.: inside lies the tomb of C. Cestius Epulones. Next to it is the **Protestant Cemetery,** running parallel to the Aurelian Walls, where P. B. Shelley, the son of Goethe and many other famous foreign poets and men of letters are buried. If we continue along the same road we come to a necropolis known as the **Sepolcro Ostiense**.

Above: *aerial view of the Porta San Paolo.*
Below: *the Pyramid of Caius Cestius (1st century B.C.).*

Basilica of St. Paul Outside the Walls

This church, the largest in the city after St. Peter's was, in July of 1823, almost completely destroyed by fire, together with its inestimable artistic treasures. It was rebuilt in 1823-29. The façade, decorated with large *mosaics*, is preceded by a large four-sided arcade. The interior, vast and majestic, consists of five naves delimited by 80 huge monolithic columns. The basilica contains a number of precious works of art: the *Triumphal Arch* with 5th century mosaics; the Gothic *ciborium* by Arnolfo di Cambio, saved from the fire, and still today in its original place above the high altar; the 13th century *mosaic* in the apse representing Christ and the Apostles; the wonderful 12th century *Paschal Candlestick* (in the Cosmatesque style, by Vassalletto); and the Chapel of the Crucifix with *frescoes* by Maderno.

Another wonderful masterpiece annexed to the basilica is its superb early 13th century **Cloister**, again the work of the Vassalletto family.

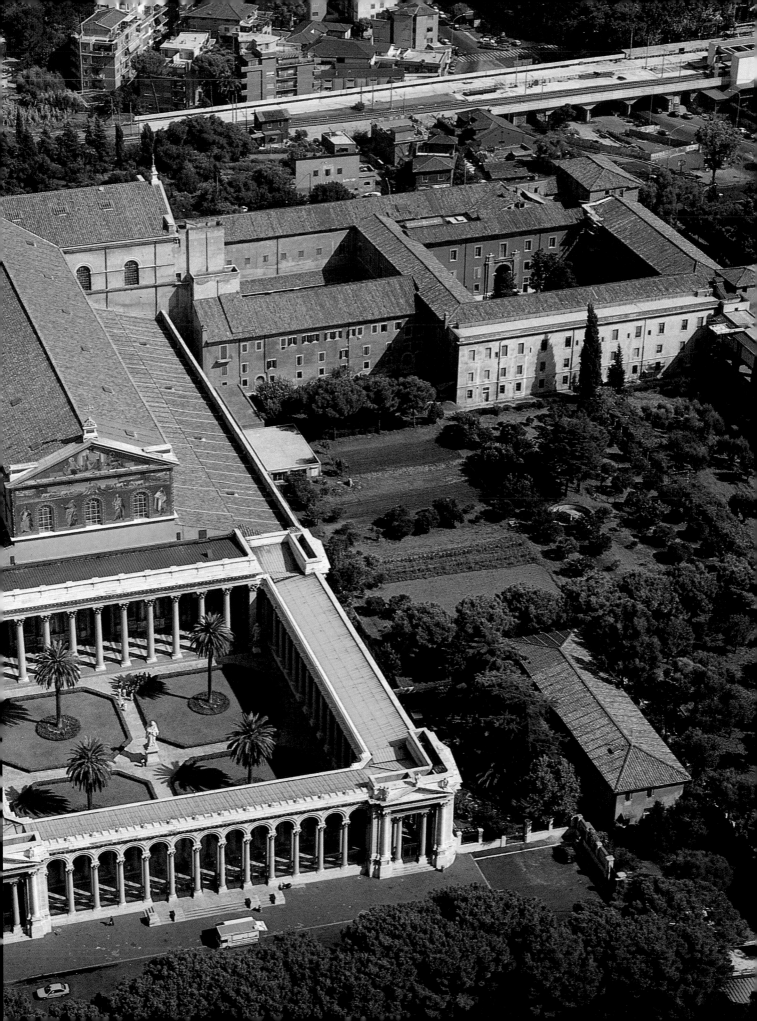

Views of the interior and the beautiful cloister of the Church of Saint Paul Outside the Walls.

E.U.R.

We now turn into the Via Laurentina, which together with the Via dell'Oceano Atlantico, the Via dell'Oceano Pacifico, the Via Ostiense and the Via delle Tre Fontane, encircles the area (420 hectares) occupied by the **E.U.R.** district. First we come to the **Abbey of the Tre Fontane,** founded, according to legend, on the site where St. Paul was decapitated. This monastic complex comprises three churches: **Santi Vincenzo ed Anastasio, Santa Maria Scala Coeli,** and **San Paolo alle Tre Fontane.** Facing the Abbey is a sanctuary visited by thousands of pilgrims each year. We now visit the E.U.R. (the initials stand for «Esposizione Universale di Roma»), the modern district designed as an exhibition centre, but unfortunately abandoned and forgotten due to the Second World War. Only in 1950 did restoration work begin, completed ten years later on the occasion of the Olympic Games in Rome. The district contains a number of public buildings: the **Palazzo dello Sport,** which can contain up to 16,000 spectators, the **Velodrome,** situated in the Viale dei Primati Sportivi, the church of **Saints Peter and Paul,** the **Palazzo della Civiltà del Lavoro,** and the **Palazzo dei Congressi.** The central Piazza Marconi is the site of some interesting museums, such as the **National Museum of Popular Arts and Traditions,** and the **Luigi Pigorini Prehistoric and Ethographic Museum.** The former contains a fascinating collection of popular goldsmith's work and various other artefacts testifying to the customs and traditions of Italian popular life in the early years of the 20th century. The other museum, also of considerable interest, is divided into two sections: Ethnographic, consisting of three rooms containing a display of ritual objects and numerous exhibits relating to various civilizations, and Prehistoric. Also worth visiting is the **Museum of Roman Civilization** (Piazza Agnelli), which houses detailed documentation of the history of Rome from its origins to the 6th century and a plastic model vividly illustrating ancient Rome.

Above: *Palazzo della Civiltà del Lavoro.*
Below: *Church of Saints Peter and Paul.*

From the Colosseum to Via Appia

From the Colosseum, by the Via San Gregorio and the Via S. Clivo di Scauro, we reach the **church of Santi Giovanni e Paolo,** very ancient in origin but almost completely restored from the Middle Ages to modern times. Continuing, we turn into the **Via S. Stefano Rotondo**, where we find the **Church**, dedicated to the saint, with its characteristic circular form. Erected in the 5th century, it contains a precious mosaic representing the *Uncrucified Christ*; the frescoes along the walls, executed in the 16th century by Pomarancio and A. Tempesta are worthy of note.

We return to the **Piazza S. Gregorio**, where the church of the same name stands; it dates back to the 6th century, but has been completely transformed in the course of the centuries.

And so we reach the area once used for chariot races and mock battles in ancient Rome: the **Circus Maximus** (2nd century B.C.). In its environs is the **Porta Capena,** one of the ancient gateways into the city, and, just beyond it, the **church of Santa Balbina** (5th century). Stretching before us are the famous **Baths of Caracalla**. This vast architectural complex, built by the emperor Caracalla in the 3rd century, consisted of a series of large rooms surrounded by delightful gardens. Inside the baths are the *frigidarium*, with its large pool; the *tepidarium* and the *calidarium*, above which was a large dome; there were, in addition, gymnasia, libraries and massage rooms. On leaving the Baths we visit the **church of San Cesareo in Palatio,** situated on the Via di Porta San Sebastiano and of very ancient origins. The church was restored by G. Della Porta in the 16th century; the interior contains some interesting Cosmatesque features as well as a fine mosaic representing *God the Father*, by F. Zucchi.

Nearby is the **Tomb of the Scipios,** a network of tunnels hewn in the rock in which the bodies of the noble Roman family, the Scipios, were laid to rest. We then come to the **Porta San Sebastiano,** more commonly known as the **Porta Appia**, beyond which the so-called «road of the catacombs» begins: the **Appia Antica.** It is along this road in fact that we find the labyrinths of passageways dug into the soft volcanic rock and used, in origin, to house the mortal remains of martyrs (who were buried in the *cubicola*), and Christian families who, on the other hand, were buried in simple niches. Later, the catacombs served as a refuge for persecuted Christians, who hid here to pray and meet together. The reasons for their persecution are to be sought in the open contradiction between the spirit of Christianity which preached equality for all and the social and economic structure of Roman society, which, in common with all ancient societies, found a ready work force in the mass of slaves (originally defeated prisoners).

Baths of Caracalla.

We now begin to explore what is in fact the oldest road of the city, opened up to provide a road link between Rome and Southern Italy.

The **church of Domine Quo Vadis?** It derives its name from the question that St. Peter, on his escape from the Mamertine prison, reputedly put to Christ: «Lord, where are you going?», he asked and the Lord replied: «I am going to Rome to be crucified a second time».

By taking the street to our right we come to the **Catacombs of St. Callixtus** - the official burial place of the bishops of Rome, they are named after Pope Callixtus who enlarged and reorganized them. They follow the **Fosse Ardeatine,** in which the Gemans, during the last war, massacred 335 Italian civilians who are buried here. In the nearby Via delle Sette Chiese are the **Catacombs of Domitilla.** They are named after Domitilla, the wife of Flavius Clemens, to whom the sepulchre above which they were laid out belonged. We now return to the Via Appia Antica to visit the **Catacombs and church of San Sebastiano.** The former are laid out on four superimposed levels and contain a bust of the Saint attributed to Bernini. Inside the church are the Chapel of the Relics, and the Albani and St. Sebastian Chapels. Then we come to the **Jewish Catacombs** and the **Catacombs of Praetextatus**. In the latter, both pagan and Christian sarcophagi are found. A short distance ahead are the **Circus of Maxentius,** built in 308, and the **Tomb of Cecilia Metella.** The latter is the best preserved of the mausolea flanking the Appian Way and is dedicated to Cecilia Metella, the wife of M. Licinius Crassus.

Above: *the Catacombs of St. Callixtus - Crypt of the Popes.*
Below: *the Catacombs of Domitilla.*

Previous page.
Above: *Porta San Sebastiano.*
Below: *Tomb of Cecilia Metella.*

The Church of San Pietro in Vincoli

It was founded by the wife of the emperor Valentinian III, Eudoxia, who wanted to preserve, in this holy place, the chains that fettered St. Peter.

Its origins are very ancient, dating back to the 5th century, but various interventions, including the 18th century restoration by Fontana, have altered it considerably. The more or less original median nave is topped by a wooden ceiling which creates a fine scenographic effect; worth noting is Parodi's fresco of *The Miracle of the Chains*. Apart from various works of art by distinguished artists such as Guercino, Domenichino and Andrea Bregno, the church contains the **Mausoleum of Julius II** by **Michelangelo.** According to the artist's design, the monument, begun on the commission of Pope Julius II in 1513, was intended to be much grander and more imposing in terms of size and the number of sculptures. It was, however, scaled down after a later agreement with the Pope, though to the great displeasure of Buonarroti, who had designed an extensive and monumental building. At the centre is the marvellous statue of *Moses* seated on a throne. The sight of this masterpiece makes a deep impression on the visitor: most striking is the expression of the face and the penetrating and angry look of the biblical patriarch as he admonishes the idolatrous Jews.

On the way up the Esquiline Hill, in the **piazza of San Martino ai Monti**, stands the **Church** dedicated to the saint, built in the first half of the 14th century.

Church of San Pietro in Vincoli with the urn (above) *containing the chains which, according to tradition, fettered St. Peter.*

Following page: *Church of San Pietro in Vincoli - the statue of Moses by Michelangelo.*

The Basilica of St. Mary Major

It is one of the major Early Christian basilicas of Rome, the only one, apart from S. Sabina, in which the subsequent modifications have not altered the original structure. According to tradition, it was built at the behest of Pope Liberius on the place where, after the apparition of the Virgin, snow had fallen in the middle of summer. In reality, it was built at the behest of Sixtus III in the 5th century. The façade executed by F. Fuga in the 18th century, consists of an elegant triple-arcaded loggia, behind which are some late-13th century mosaics representing the above-cited miracle. The interior, with three naves, is striking for its beauty and solemnity, thanks also to the sumptuous *coffered ceiling* over the great nave, perhaps the work of G. Sangallo, carried out, according to tradition, using the first gold to be brought back from America. Noteworthy too is the *Cosmatesque floor* (12th century). Above the entablature are some precious 5th century mosaics representing various episodes from the Bible; in the apse is J. Torriti's splendid mosaic of the *Triumph of Mary*. The basilica contains the **oratory of the Crib** with statues by A. Di Cambio, the fine 18th century *baldacchino* by Fuga and a number of chapels: the Sistine Chapel executed by D. Fontana in the 16th century; it contains a *ciborium* in the shape of a temple by L. Scalzo; the Pauline or Borghese Chapel built by F. Ponzio in the 17th century containing frescoes by Reni and the Cavalier d'Arpino; the Sforza Chapel, built by G. della Porta after a design by Michelangelo. The Basilica is flanked by a Romanesque bell-tower: the highest in Rome (75 m.).

From the Piazza Santa Maria Maggiore we continue along the Via Merulana, where a short distance ahead to the right we can visit **the church of Santa Prassede.** Erected in the 5th century, and subsequently completely rebuilt, it has undergone, in the course of the ensuing centuries, various alterations and enlargements. It contains some splendid *mosaics* of the 9th century. The Chapel of St. Zeno, an important monument of the Byzantine period in Rome, also dates to this period. The bones of St. Praxed and her sister St. Pudentiana, and many other Christian relics, are preserved in this church.

Before continuing our itinerary, let us make our way round to the back of the Basilica of St. Mary Major (Piazza dell'Esquilino) to visit the **church of Santa Pudenziana**, of ancient origins, but recently transformed, in whose interior various works dating back to the original period are preserved; worthy of note is the mosaic in the apse of the 4th century representing *Christ among the Apostles*.

Basilica of St. Mary Major.

Above: *the back facade.*

Below: *Detail of the front facade with the bell-tower.*

We now take the Via Carlo Alberto, which leads us to the **church of Sant'Antonio** and the **Arch of Gallienus**. A short distance ahead lies the large Piazza Vittorio Emanuele II, from where, by way of the Via Mamiani, we reach the long thoroughfare of G. Giolitti, one end of which terminates at the Railway Station (**Stazione Termini**) and the Piazza dei Cinquecento facing it, and the other at the Piazza di Porta Maggiore. From the station we take Via S. Bibiana to visit the **Basilica of St. Laurence Outside the Walls.**

The church was erected by Constantine who wanted to build a sacred shrine over the site where St. Laurence had been martyred. Later, in the 6th century, Pelagio II, had another building with a square plan constructed close to the first and in the 13th century at the behest of Onorio III, the two buildings were joined together into a single basilica. Worth noting in the interior are the 13th century *episcopal throne,* the 12th century *ciborium,* the two *ambos* and the *mosaic* on the triumphal arch from the 6th century. A few steps from the Basilica is the **Cemetery of Campo Verano**, where many celebrated personalities are buried; here lies the tomb of E. Petrolini on which the fol-

lowing inscription appears: "From out of your mouth, sang the soul of Rome". From the Piazza San Lorenzo, where the second highest **column** in Rome stands, after that of the **Immaculata** in the Piazza di Spagna, we can take the Via C. De Lollis to visit the **University City**. This extensive campus, built in the nineteen thirties contains some interesting museums, including the **Museum of Origins,** with exhibits relating to various geological eras, and the **Museum of Mineralogy.**

Following the Via dei Fori Imperiali (again starting out from the Piazza Venezia), and circling the Colosseum, we reach the Via San Giovanni in Laterano on which the **church of San Clemente** is situated. The basilica in fact consists of two superimposed churches: the upper one with a fine baroque façade by Fontana and a lower one (4th century), interred below ground to permit the construction of the later church built over it (12th century). The interior of the upper church, remodelled in the 17th century, has a nave and two aisles divided by ancient columns. It contains a 12th century *schola cantorum*; a 12th century mosaic of the *Triumph of the Cross* in the apse; and 15th century *frescoes* by Masolino da

Panicale in the Chapel of St. Catherine of Alexandria. From the sacristy we descend to the lower basilica which retains a series of valuable frescoes. Nearby, at the beginning of the Via dei **Quattro Santi Coronati**, is the church of the same name, dating back to the 4th century but variously transformed. Of particular interest is its fine early 13th century Cloister. The **church** itself preserves its ancient granite columns and *Cosmatesque floor*. Below is a Crypt where the relics of some martyr saints are preserved. We continue to the Piazza San Giovanni in Laterano, at the centre of which stands the **Egyptian Obelisk,** the tallest of the thirteen obelisks extant in Rome. Brought here from the Circus Maximus in 1588, it dates to the 15th century B.C. To its right is the **Lateran Baptistery,** which has ancient origins; it was erected by Constantine. At the centre of its polygonal interior is a large font in green basalt in which the sacrament of baptism was administered by immersion. It is surrounded by a colonnade of porphyry columns supporting a cornice with smaller white marble columns above, and four chapels with wonderful *mosaics* dating from the 5th and 7th centuries.

Basilica of St. Mary Major: the eighteenth century baldacchino by Fuga.

The Basilica of St. John Lateran

Following page: *the Tabernacle in the Basilica of St. John Lateran.*

Basilica of St. John Lateran - exterior.

We now visit the Basilica of St. John Lateran, second only to St. Peter's in importance. It was erected at the beginning of the 4th century over an area of the family palace of the Laterani donated to the church by the emperor Constantine. Damaged by fires and earthquakes, sacked during the barbarian invasions, the basilica has been continuously reconstructed, enlarged and enriched with precious decorations and works of art. It was extensively remodelled in the baroque style by Borromini in the 17th century. Its main façade was raised in the 18th century by Alessandro Galilei: simple and yet majestic, it consists of a single order of huge pilasters supporting a ponderous entablature with a balustrade above, topped, against the skyline, by *15 statues of Christ and flanking saints*. Below is the portico, providing access to the five entrances to the basilica. The middle one has *Roman bronze doors* brought from the Curia in the Roman Forum; the one to the far right is the **Porta Santa**.

The huge interior is divided into a nave and four aisles. The nave is topped by a sumptuous gilt *wooden ceiling* (16th century), and has a fine *Cosmatesque floor*. Large niches containing *statues of the 12 Apostles* are placed between the piers of the nave. Among the treasures contained in the basilica, we may cite: the magnificent **tabernacle** placed over the papal altar sculpted in the gothic style by Giovanni di Stefano in the 14th century and enshrining the heads of Saints Peter and Paul; the delicately carved bronze *tomb-slab* of Martin V; the transept restored by G. Della Porta, decorated with *frescoes* which are genuine masterpieces of 16th century art (part of the frescoes were damaged by the terrorist attack of 1993); the apse with a 13th century *mosaic* by J. Turriti and J. da Camerino. On the first pillar to the right of the middle nave is the fragment of a fresco attributed to Giotto, *Boniface VIII proclaiming the Jubilee*. In the Corsini Chapel: a sumptuous work by A. Galilei, executed in 1734. From the back of the left-hand nave the visitor can gain access to the beautiful Cosmatesque **Cloister,**

the work of the Vassalletto family. On the right flank of the basilica is the **Lateran Palace.** Pope Sixtus V commissioned the architect D. Fontana in 1586 to reconstruct it over the former papal palace - the gift of Constantine - with the intention of establishing the summer residence of the Popes in it; an aim that was never realized. The palace has also housed the Christian, Profane and Missionary Ethnological collections, which have now been transferred to the Vatican. The interior, recently restored, is richly frescoed (the painters involved in its decoration included Baldassarre Croce, C. Nebbia and G. B. Ricci).

In a building on the other side of the piazza is the **Scala Santa:** the staircase which, according to tradition, was ascended by Christ on his way to Pilate.

The building was erected by D. Fontana in the 16th century to house the **Chapel of St. Laurence:** the papal chapel. Richly decorated with works of art, the chapel contains relics of great value and for this reason is known as the **Sancta Sanctorum.** Over the altar is the Miraculous Image of *Jesus Christ*, so-called because it is thought to have been "painted by a non-human hand". In the piazza facing the church of St. John Lateran is a *Monument to St. Francis of Assisi.* The Porta San Giovanni marks the starting point of the Via Appia Nuovo, by means of which we can reach the **Castelli Romani** (Castelgandolfo, summer residence of the Pope; Marino, Albino and Frascati, famous for their typical wines). From the Piazza San Giovanni in Laterano we now take the Viale Carlo Felice to

the Piazza **Santa Croce in Gerusalemme** on which the **Church** of the same name stands, dating back to the 4th century, but completely remodelled in the baroque period. It contains the *relic of the Cross of Jesus Christ* from which it derives its name. A short distance away is the Piazza Porta Maggiore where we find the **Porta Maggiore** (erected by Claudius in 52 A.D.) and the **Basilica** of the same name. The latter, underground, was only recently discovered (1917). It can be dated to the early years of the 1st century A.D. It contains a number of notable wall paintings.

We can conclude our itinerary by visiting the **Catacombs of Marcellinus and Petrus,** which can be reached by way of the Via Casilina, which starts from outside the Porta Maggiore.

The Scala Santa.

The Chapel of St. Laurence or Sancta Sanctorum.

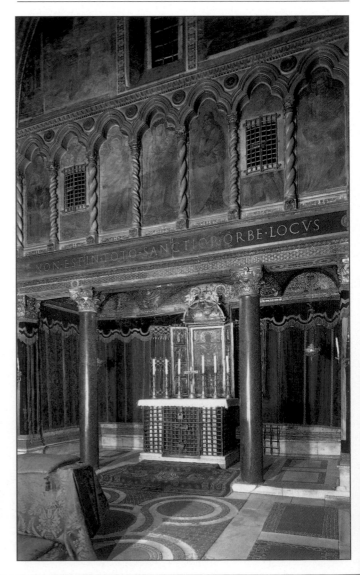

Piazza Colonna

Let us now visit the **Palazzo Colonna** (reachable by way of the Via C. Battisti and then by the Via IV Novembre). it was built at the behest of Martin V in the 15th century, and restored, in its present form, in the 18th century.

The linearity and simplicity of the building's external structure is at variance with the pomp and sumptuousness that characterize its inner rooms. The **Colonna Gallery,** laid out in three grandiose rooms, comprises an interesting collection of paintings including: *Narcissus*, by **Tintoretto;** *Portrait of G. Colonna,* by **Van Dyck**; *Apollo and Daphne,* by **N. Poussin;** *Guidobaldo da Montefeltro* by **Melozzo da Forlì**. Further on we come to the Markets of Trajan, adjacent to which rises the 13th century Torre delle Milizie and the 17th century church of Santa Caterina. We continue along the Via Nazionale (Vicus Longus), always crowded with people, to the **Palazzo delle Esposizioni,** built in the 19th century after a design by the architect Pio Piacentini, in which the ***Quadrennial Exhibition*** is held.

Next to it is the **church of San Vitale** built in the 5th century, but remodelled in subsequent periods; the portal of the façade, in the 15th century style, bears the coat of arms of Sixtus IV. Next is the **church of St. Paul's,** with valuable frescoes inside. In the Via Firenze, on the way to Piazza Esedra stands the **Opera House.**

PIAZZA ESEDRA

The large piazza is dominated at its centre by the famous **Fountain of the Naiads,** representing the *Nymph of the underground waters*, borne on a dragon, the *Nymph of the oceans,* the *Nymph of the rivers*, and lastly the *Nymph of the lakes* with a swan. The central figure is that of *Glaucus* who dominates the forces of nature.

Piazza Esedra (Piazza della Repubblica) with its beautiful Fountain of the Naiads.

CHURCH OF SANTA MARIA DEGLI ANGELI

Situated in the Piazza Esedra, it was designed by Michelangelo in the 16th century, using the ruins belonging to the nearby Baths of Diocletian. In the 18th century, however, Vanvitelli was called to build the Chapel of St. Nicola Albergati, thus modifying the interior's original appearance as designed by Michelangelo. The church is full of works of art, including the *Punishment of Ananias* by **Pomarancio**, the *Crucifixion of St. Peter* by **N. Ricciolini**, the *Martyrdom of St. Sebastian*, by **Domenichino**, and *The Mass of St. Basil* by **P. Subleyras**. A number of interesting funerary monuments are also contained in the church, such as those of Cardinals Alciati and Parisi, and those of Salvator Rosa and Carlo Maratta.

The **Baths of Diocletian** house the **Museo Nazionale Romano**. Founded in 1889, the museum contains numerous works of Greek and Roman sculpture, sarcophagi, terracottas and paintings. In the Room of the Masterpieces are displayed the *Diskobolos of Castel Porziano*, a copy of Myron's original in bronze, and the *Niobe of the Orti Sallustiani*; the Ludovisi collection comprises among its 102 sculptures: *The dying Gaul with his wife, Aphrodite* and the *Ares Ludovisi*.

Following page: *the Quirinal.*

Church of Santa Maria degli Angeli: a sixteenth century building modified in the 18th century by Vanvitelli.

THE QUIRINAL

We now make our way back down the Via Nazionale, until we come to the Piazza Magnapoli, from where we continue along the Via XXIV Maggio, on which the **Villa Colonna** and the **church of San Silvestro al Quirinale** are situated. The latter, erected in the 11th century, was completely transformed in the 16th. Close by is the **Palazzo Rospigliosi Pallavicini,** built in 1603: it contains a famous **Gallery** containing paintings by Caravaggio, Rubens, Botticelli, Raphael and other illustrious artists. Its garden pavilion, the **Casino dell'Aurora,** is decorated with a beautiful *ceiling fresco* by Guido Reni. We have now arrived in the **Piazza del Quirinale** dominated by its magnificent **Fountain of the Dioscuri.**

The **Quirinal Palace,** begun in the 16th century as a summer residence for the Popes, completed in the 18th century by such distinguished architects as Bernini, Fontana and Maderno, takes its name from the hill on which it

stands: the Quirinal. Worthy of note is the arcaded courtyard, at the far end of which is the clock-tower and the mosaic depicting the *Virgin Mary* based on a design by Maratta. The sumptuously decorated inner rooms are adorned with frescoes by Maratta, Reni and other distinguished artists, and in addition are hung with 16th and 17th century *tapestries*. The palace is now the official residence of the President of the Republic.

The piazza is also home to the **Palazzo della Consulta,** built to the design of F. Fuga in the 18th century, and now the seat of Italy's Constitutional Court. Further ahead is the **church of Sant'Andrea al Quirinale,** a masterpiece by Bernini who built it in 1671.

Its interior, elliptical in form, is decorated with beautiful frescoed chapels and polychrome marbles; worth mentioning is Borgognone's *Crucifixion* (high altar).

A short way ahead stands the **church of San Carlo alle Quattro Fontane**, a masterpiece by Borromini.

PALAZZO BARBERINI

We now turn into the Via delle Quattro Fontane, so-called on account of the four fountains placed at the corners, until we arrive in **Piazza Barberini** with Bernini's graceful **Fountain of the Triton**. Adjacent is the **Palazzo Barberini,** considered among the most sumptuous palaces of the Roman nobility. Erected by Maderno in the 17th century, it was completed by Borromini and Bernini. On opposite sides of the entrance are, to the right, a magnificent spiral staircase by Borromini and, to the left, the grand staircase by Bernini.

Inside on the first floor we find the large hall with its famous fresco of the *Triumph of the Barberini* which Pietro da Cortona executed on the ceiling. In the past the palace housed the Barberini Gallery, rich in extremely valuable works of art and a Library of over 60,000 books, subsequently acquired for the Vatican Library. It now houses the **Galleria Nazionale di Arte Antica** which includes paintings by

Above: *the dome of the Church of San Carlo alle Quattro Fontane.*
Below: *Church of San Carlo alle Quattro Fontane: the cloister.*

Raphael (*La Fornarina*); Fra Angelico (*Triptych*); Tintoretto and Perugino.

Having left the palace we come to Bernini's charming **Fountain of the Bees,** which marks the beginning of the elegant **Via Vittorio Veneto**, lined with luxury hotels, shops and cosmopolitan cafès where it is possible to meet famous people from the world of culture and entertainment, and along which it is agreeable to stroll in order to drink in not only the charm of a city where, still today, you can stumble across a picturesque corner, street or bar, but also the atmosphere, which Rome itself exudes, lost in your thoughts and memories.

Nearby are the **church of Santa Maria della Concezione** or **church of the Capuchins,** built in the 17th century and containing Reni's *The Archangel St. Michael* and Caravaggio's beautiful *St. Francis*, among others; the **church of Sant'Isidoro** and finally the **Palazzo Margherita,** dedicated to the Queen and now the American Embassy.

Above: *View of Palazzo Barberini.*
Below: *the Fountain of the Triton.*

From Castro Pretorio to Via Nomentana and Via Salaria

Another fascinating tour through the streets of the city is the one to Castro Pretorio, Porta Pia and, along the Via Salaria and Via Nomentana, to the Villa Torlonia, bearing in mind the many churches, palaces and piazzas we will encounter along our route. We set out from the Piazza Barberini, until, we reach, by way of the street of the same name, the piazza San Bernardo with the two **churches of San Bernardo and Santa Susanna** (17th century).

Continuing along the Via XX Settembre, we come, on the right (Via Goito), to the **Castro Pretorio** before reaching the **Porta Pia**. This gateway, famous for the episode of the taking of Rome, was designed by Michelangelo and built by Della Porta.

We now continue along the Via Nomentana, flanked by rich and famous historic villas: **Paganini, Mirafiori, Torlonia, Agnese** and, on the Via Salaria, **Albani, Chigi** and **Ada**.

The first one to take into consideration is without doubt the **Villa Torlonia,** with its twin *obelisks*. Begun by Valadier and completed by Caretti, it was the property of the banker G. Torlonia who wanted to create a splendid residence amidst lawns and palm-trees. Further along is the **Basilica of St. Agnes Outside the Walls,** built in 342 over the Catacombs in which the mortal remains of the Saint were preserved, and the **church of Santa Costanza**, a distinctive circular Early Christian building, which contains some fine 4th century mosaics.

We return to the Porta Pia and, by way of the Corso Italia, reach Piazza Fiume, whence begins the **Via Salaria**. Situated on this major road are the **Villa Chigi,** built for Cardinal F. Chigi; the **Villa Ada,** formerly the property of the House of Savoy; and the **Villa Albani**. The latter initially housed a valuable collection of ancient art, later acquired by A. Torlonia together with the villa. The two finest buildings of the complex are the **Casino** and the **Caféhaus,** set amid a beautiful park of pines, cedars and sequoias. Inside is an interesting collection of paintings by Perugino, Tintoretto, Guercino and other illustrious artists. Also on the Via Salaria are the **Catacombs of Priscilla,** considered the most important in the city, and definitely worth a visit. Beyond the Aniene river is the district of **Montesacro**.

Church of Santa Costanza - early Christian basilica with a circular plan.

Following page.
Above: *the Basilica of St. Agnes Outside the Walls*

Below: *Villa Ada.*

The Trevi Fountain

Starting from the Piazza Venezia, we take the Via C. Battisti to the **Basilica of the Santi Apostoli** (4th century). Modernized by Fontana and Valadier in the 18th century, reinterpreting the facade in the Neo-classical style, it houses the beautiful Chapel of the Crucifix and other valuable works of art. From the nearby Piazza della Pilotta, we take the Via San Vincenzo Lucchesi which leads us to the spectacular **Trevi Fountain.** Erected for Clement XII by the architect N. Salvi towards the end of the 17th century, it shows at its centre the statue of *Ocean* riding in a chariot drawn by two *Tritons*. Into the basin below, symbolizing the sea, it is the time-honoured custom to throw a coin to guarantee a return to this splendid city. Nearby is the **Academy of St. Luke** (Palazzo Carpegna), seat of an interesting exhibition of works by Reni, Guercino, Titian, Van Dyck and others.

We then emerge onto the Via del Tritone, a bustling modern thoroughfare, full of boutiques and crowded with shoppers at all times of the day. Turning off to the left (along the Via Nazareno) we can visit the **church of Sant'Andrea delle Fratte,** flanked by Borromini's graceful brick belfry: it is nicknamed the «campanile ballerino» due to the slight oscillations it registers whenever the bells are rung.

The Trevi Fountain: perhaps the most famous and spectacular of Rome's fountains.

The Piazza di Spagna

Elegant and scenic, the Piazza di Spagna provides a welcoming point of encounter at the centre of Rome. Its peculiar fascination derives from a combination of colour, the 18th century buildings that surround it, the flowers that adorn the **Spanish Steps**, and the animated and cosmopolitan atmosphere that pervades it. From this piazza fan out such prestigious streets as the **Via Margutta,** famous because of the many painters who live and display their works there; the **Via del Babuino,** with its many antique shops; the **Via Condotti,** with its sophisticated boutiques and celebrated **Caffè Greco,** dating back to the 18th century, a historic place of rendezvous of great Italian and foreign artists; the **Via Borgognona,** it too flanked by fashionable boutiques and couturiers; and the lively **Via Frattina.** At the centre of the Piazza di Spagna is placed a marvellous fountain in the shape of a boat: the **Fontana della Barcaccia,** designed by Pietro Bernini, father of the more famous Gian Lorenzo, who was the architect, in part, of the nearby **Palazzo di Propaganda Fide:** he was responsible for the façade looking onto the piazza, while the lateral elevation was by Borromini. Yet the soul of the piazza consists of the **Spanish Steps** which rise from it. Designed by Francesco De Sanctis in the early years of the 18th century, this elegant staircase ascends in three ramps from the piazza, interrupted by terraces, the last and most scenic of which is the one with the balustrade on top: the Piazza Trinità dei Monti with its obelisk, formerly in the gardens of Sallust on the Quirinal and set up here in 1789. Always thronged with young people and foreigners, with pictures by the painters of Via Margutta and its flower stall, the Spanish Steps are enlivened each May by a display of azaleas from the municipal greenhouses. At the top of the Steps is the **church of the Trinità dei Monti,** built in the 16th century on behalf of the French king Louis XII. The façade, by C. Maderno, projecting upwards with its two symmetrical bell-towers either side, is approached by a flight of stairs designed by Fontana.

Above: *Piazza di Spagna and the Fontana della Barcaccia.*
Below: *the Church of the Trinità dei Monti.*

Villa Borghese – Borghese Museum and Gallery

We are now on the Pincian Hill, and by turning left into the Viale Trinità dei Monti, we come to the **Villa Medici.** Built in the 16th century, it passed into the hands of France during the 19th century and later became the seat of the **French Academy,** established by Louis XIV for all young Frenchman wishing to develop their knowledge of art. We now enter the **Pincio,** the magnificent public park laid out by Valadier in the early years of the 19th century, from where we can enjoy a marvellous view of the city, particularly lovely at sunset.

Continuing our walk, we enter the extensive park of the **Villa Borghese,** full of centuries-old trees, extensive lawns, cool lakes and fountains. All this makes a wonderful setting for the **Palazzo Borghese** itself, which was built for Cardinal Scipione Borghese by Vasanzio between 1613 and 1615. It now houses the **Borghese Museum and Gallery.** The Borghese Gallery is without doubt the first Museum created with the express purpose of housing artistic masterpieces.

Both the building, that is the so-called Casino Borghese, and the Museum and Gallery were restored and reopened to the public in June 1997 after almost 14 years of patient and painstaking work, which has led to the complete reorganization of the art collection according to more functional criteria as well as taking into better account the exhibition space.

All the rooms in the Borghese Museum are richly decorated and contain, ranged along the walls, ancient statues and marble fragments. The rooms house some of the greatest masterpieces of Italian sculpture of the 17th and 18th centuries. In the other rooms: the enchanting *Venus Victrix*, a portrait of ***Paolina Borghese***, sister of Napoleon and wife of Prince C. Borghese, a wonderful work by **A. Canova**; *David*, a famous statue executed in his early period by **G. L. Bernini** for Cardinal S. *Borghese: Apollo and Daphne,* the group of *Aeneas and Anchises* and *The Rape of Proserpine* are by the same artist.

In the **Gallery of the Emperors,** there are 18 busts of emperors dating to the 17th century.

There is a rich and valuable collection of paintings including *Saints Cosmas and Damian* by **D. Dossi, Raphael's** *Deposition, Sacred and Profane Love* by **Titian,** and *The Portrait of a Man* by **Messina.** In addition there are six works by **Caravaggio**: *The Madonna dei Palafrenieri, David with the head of Goliath, St. John the Baptist, The sick Bacchus, Youth with a basket of fruit* and *St. Jerome.* In addition there are other admirable works by **Pinturicchio, Botticelli** and **Rubens.**

Returning outside, close to the Palazzo Borghese, we come to the **Zoological Garden,** founded in 1911, and, on the Via Aldrovandi, the **Civic Museum of Zoology** and the **African Museum.**

Villa Medici.

Villa Borghese: Piazza di Siena (above) *and an atmospheric view of the Temple of Aesculapius.*

Left-hand page: *the exterior and one of the rooms inside the Borghese Gallery.*

Above: *David hurling a stone from his sling and Apollo and Daphne (statue by Bernini).*

Below: *Paolina Bonaparte, a famous statue by Antonio Canova.*

The latter contains some interesting exhibits illustrating the history and traditions of Africa. Continuing along the Via Aldrovandi, we come to the Valle Giulia in which the Palazzo delle Belle Arti is situated, and which houses the **National Gallery of Modern Art,** founded in 1883. Here we can admire works by the greatest names in Italian and foreign painting and sculpture of the 19th and 20th centuries: among the neoclassical artists, **Canova;** among the artists of the Romantic school, **Hayez** and **Segantini;** among the Macchiaoli (Italian impressionists), **Fattori** and **Signorini;** and then **Degas, Monet, Cézanne, Van Gogh, Modigliani, Mafai, De Chirico, Guttuso and Burri.**

We now take the Viale delle Belle Arti on which the Villa of Pope Julius II stands, which houses the **National Museum of Villa Giulia,** comprising rich and wideranging archaeological artefacts of the pre-Roman period, found during excavations carried out in the regions of Central Italy.

Among the various grave goods, statues and reconstructions of tombs on display, we find the wonderful Etruscan terracotta sculpture: ***Sarcophagus of the «Married Couple».***

Left-hand page:
Borghese Gallery: Madonna of the Pomegranate (S. Botticelli); Leda and the Swan (Leonardo da Vinci); Youth with a basket of fruit (Caravaggio); Sibyl (Dominichino).

Villa Borghese: Modern art gallery (above) and Villa Giulia (below): both buildings house museums of great artistic and documentary interest.

Villa Giulia National Museum: detail of the Sarcophagus of the Married Couple (above).

Below: *Apollo of Veius, a splendid example of Etruscan art of the 5th-6th century B.C.*

Following page: *Piazza del Popolo.*

The Via del Corso is a long straight street linking the Piazza Venezia with the Piazza del Popolo. It is flanked by many imposing palaces built in various periods and in various styles. Starting out once again from the Piazza Venezia, we find, to the left, on the corner of the Corso, the 17th century **Palazzo Bonaparte** (where Napoleon's mother lived). It is followed, on the opposite side of the Corso, by the **Palazzo Salviati,** baroque in style, and the **Palazzo Odescalchi** (19th century). Opposite is the large **Palazzo Doria,** containing the **Doria Pamphilj Gallery:** a magnificent private collection of works of art including such masterpieces as: *Spain succouring Religion* by **Titian;** *Portrait of a Prelate* by **Tintoretto;** *Rest during the Flight into Egypt* and *Mary Magdalen,* youthful works by **Caravaggio;** *St. Sebastian* by **Ludovico Carracci;** *Portrait of Innocent X* by **Velazquez;** *Madonna and Child* by **Parmigianino;** and *Bust of Innocent X* by **Bernini.** Adjacent to the palace is the **church of Santa Maria in Via Lata,** of very ancient origins, but subjected to numerous alterations and restorations during the 11th, 15th and 17th centuries. The existing *baroque facade* is by Pietro da Cortona. The interior, with a nave and two aisles, is notable for its beautiful high *altar* adorned with alabaster columns, attributed to Bernini.

On the Via Lata on the corner of the church is a little fountain known as the **Fountain of the Porter,** another of the «speaking statues» of Rome. Continuing along this street we come to the **Collegio Romano** (16th century). The building, designed by Bartolomeo Ammannati, was in the past an important college run by the Jesuits.

The **church of San Marcello,** situated on the Corso, dates back to the early years of the 4th century, but in the 16th century was devastated by a fire which destroyed every trace of the original building. The existing structure is by Iacopo Sansovino, while the *baroque facade* was designed by Carlo Fontana. Facing it is the **Palace of the Banco di Roma,** an 18th century building by Alessandro Specchi. It is followed by the **Palace of the Cassa di Risparmio** by Antonio Cipolla and, on the opposite side of the Corso, the **Palazzo Sciarra Colonna** (16th century). Nearby is the **church of Sant'Ignazio di Loyola,** reachable by taking the Via Caravita. It was designed by the Jesuit father Orazio

Grassi, on the basis of earlier designs by Carlo Maderno. The lavish baroque interior was decorated by Andrea Pozzo, who also frescoed the imposing vault over the nave. By way of the Via dei Burrò we reach the Piazza di Pietra, in which an imposing row of columns is all that remains of the **Temple of Hadrian.** From here we make our way into the nearby Piazza Colonna, dominated by the *Column of Marcus Aurelius,* similar in structure to Trajan's Column and erected in 180-196. The Piazza is flanked by the **Palazzo della Galleria Colonna,** the **Palazzo Ferraioli** and the **church of San Bartolomeo dei Bergamaschi;** the *fountain* is by Giacomo Della Porta (16th century). At the centre of the adjacent Piazza Montecitorio is the **obelisk of Psammeticus II,** raised here by Pius VI in 1792. Facing it is the **Palazzo Montecitorio,** begun by Bernini in 1650 and completed by Carlo Fontana. The building is now the seat of Italy's Chamber of Deputies.

In the Piazza Colonna, we come to the facade of the **Palazzo Chigi,** a 16th century work by G. Della Porta and S. Maderno. The building, extended by the Genga brothers, is now the office of the Prime Minister. On Via del Tritone is the **church of Santa Maria in Via,** dating back to the 10th century; the facade, executed by Rainaldi, is much later however (16th century). The **Caffè Aragno** is worth mentioning: dating to 1870, it was a famous rendezvous for the intellectual and political élite of the time. In the Piazza di San Lorenzo in Lucina we can visit the **church of San Lorenzo,** founded between the end of the 4th and the beginning of the 5th century and reconstructed in c. 1100, the period to which the beautiful bell-tower and the portico belong.

Continuing along the Corso, we see the 16th century **Palazzo Ruspoli** and, just beyond it, the **church of Santi Ambrogio e Carlo al Corso,** built by Onorio Longhi in the period 1612 to 1672 and subsequently completed by his son Martino. The huge dome, however, was designed by P. da Cortona. Having reached the end of the Via del Corso, we enter the **Piazza del Popolo**: an admirable work by G. Valadier, who laid it out at the beginning of the 19th century. The piazza opens at the confluence of the Via di Ripetta, the Via del Corso and the Via del Babuino. At its entrance are the **twin churches** of **Santa Maria di Monte-**santo and **Santa Maria dei Miracoli,** erected in the 17th century. After the initial work by Carlo Rainaldi, they were completed by Bernini and Fontana. Two hemicycles enclose the Piazza, which on one side is flanked by the Pincian Hill. At the centre is the **Flaminian Obelisk:** constructed in Egypt in the 13th century B.C. it was brought to Rome by desire of Augustus.

The basins and lions at the base are the work of Valadier. The piazza terminates at the Porta del Popolo and, on the right, is the church of S. Maria del Popolo, which wonderfully completes the scenic ensemble.

Church of S. Maria del Popolo

The church arose over an ancient chapel built, in the late 11th century, at public expense (according to some, it is this fact that gave rise to its name). Following an enlargement in the 13th century, it assumed its present Renaissance appearance. The prolongation of the apse was the work of Bramante. The interior with three naves and a Latin cross plan displays the restorations in the baroque style carried out by Bernini.

The church contains works of art of considerable importance: the 1st chapel in the right nave is decorated with frescoes by Pinturicchio and works by A. Bregno, Mino da Fiesole and F. Sangallo; in the Cybo Chapel by C. Fontana we can admire a painting by C. Maratto; in the Great Chapel are the *monuments* of Cardinal G. Basso Della Rovere and Cardinal Ascanio Sforza, the work of A. Sansovino; on the altar: *Madonna del Popolo* (13th century); in the left transept *Con-*version *of St. Paul* and the *Crucifixion of St. Peter* by Caravaggio; the Chigi Chapel was designed by Raphael, who also designed the mosaics in the cupola. Adjacent to the church is the **Porta del Popolo,** at one time the Porta Flaminia. It was constructed in 1561, based on a design by Michelangelo and Vignola. The facade looking onto the piazza is by Bernini who modified it into an honorary arch for the entrance of Maria Christina of Sweden.

The Piazzale Flaminio, to the right of which is the main entrance to the Villa Borghese, marks the start of the Via Flaminia, which ever since antiquity has linked Rome with Rimini.

On this road, at the junction with the Viale delle Belle Arti, is the **Palazzina of Pius IV,** whose design is perhaps attributable to Vignola. A short distance away is the **Chapel of Sant'Andrea** by Vignola. We now come to the **Flaminian Stadium,** erected in 1960 by the architect Nervi on the occasion of the Olympic Games. Other sports grounds and facilities were laid out in the same area. In its environs is the modern residential quarter of **Parioli.** From the Viale dei Parioli we can reach the source of the **Acqua Acetosa,** an excellent mineral water. Continuing along the Via Flaminia, we come to the **Ponte Milvio,** known as the Ponte Molle, which dates to the 2nd century B.C.

In the area between Monte Mario and the Tiber is the **Foro Italico.** This houses one of the largest and best-equipped sports centres. It includes the Marmi Stadium and the Olympic Stadium.

The Church of Santa Maria sopra Minerva

From the Piazza Venezia, by way of the Via del Plebiscito, we reach the Piazza del Gesù, from where we turn right into the Via del Gesù and so arrive in the Piazza Minerva. At the centre of the piazza is a small **Egyptian obelisk** (6th century B.C.) supported on the back of Bernini's marble *Elephant*. To the right is the **church of Santa Maria sopra Minerva.** Erected in the 8th century over the ruins of a temple dedicated to Minerva, the church has undergone various alterations and restorations. Its spacious interior is notable for its fine chapels containing some valuable works of art. We may mention, among the many: the Chapel of the Annunziata in the right aisle, designed by Carlo Maderno with a fine altarpiece by Antoniazzo Romano depicting *The Annunciation*; the Carafa Chapel in the right transept with wonderful frescoes by Filippino Lippi (1488-92) and *tombs* by Giuliano da Maiano and Giacomo Cosma (*tomb of Guglielmo Durand* by Giacomo Cosma); the Aldobrandini Chapel by G. Della Porta and C. Maderno with the monuments to the parents of Clement VIII by Della Porta; in the presbytery the sculpture of the *Redeemer* by Michelangelo; behind the high altar are the funerary monuments of Clement VII and Leo X designed by Sangallo; the *tomb* of F. Tornabuoni by Mino da Fiesole; the *tomb of Cardinal D. Coca* by A. Bregno; on the penultimate pillar of the left-hand nave a *monument* by Bernini to Maria Reggi (1643).

Church of Santa Maria sopra Minerva: view of the exterior and the interior. Above left: the statue of the Redeemer by Michelangelo.

The Pantheon

The Pantheon is one of the most important and most imposing of Roman temples: it is also the best preserved. It was built by Marcus Agrippa, son-in-law of Augustus, in 27 B.C., in honour of all the gods: hence its name.

Destroyed by a fire in 80 A.D., it was rebuilt in the time of Hadrian (between 110 and 125 A.D.). In 609 the temple was consecrated as a Christian church by Pope Boniface IV, who dedicated it to the Virgin Mary and all the Martyr Saints. The church became the burial place of illustrious Italian artists, such as Raphael Sanzio, the architects Baldassarre Peruzzi and Vignola, the painter Annibale Caracci, and also members of Italy's royal family: the Kings of Italy Victor Emanuel II and Umberto I and Queen Margherita. It is the only Roman temple which, after having been used for Christian worship, did not undergo transformations to its structure: although in fact the plaster and bronze decorations and the bronze covering of the dome were removed.

It is circular in plan, covered by a dome whose diameter is equal to its height, and preceded by a gabled pronaos of Greek type supported by sixteen granite columns surmounted by Corinthian capitals.

We enter the temple through an imposing bronze portal of Roman date.

The interior is majestic and highly original: rectangular alternating with semicircular niches are laid out round its walls; the hemispherical dome, of exceptional diameter (43.30 metres; equal to its height from the floor), is decorated with coffering and illuminated by a central aperture some 9 metres in diameter.

With regard to its constructional technique, it seems that the skeleton of the dome consists of a series of ribs whose weight is supported on the massive arches situated in the parts of the cylindrical walls not opened by the large niches.

This and other architectural solutions make the Pantheon a wonderful monumental work in which grandeur of mass and gracefulness of line combine to form an awe-inspiring cohesion of effect.

Pantheon: built at the behest of Augustus in 27 B.C. in honour of all the gods and one of the most important and magnificent Roman temples.

The **church of San Luigi dei Francesi,** reachable by the Via Giustiniani, was erected in the 16th century by Fontana; its interior houses important works by Caravaggio. In the street running parallel to it, the Corso del Rinascimento, is the Palazzo Madama, the seat of the Italian Senate since 1870, decorated with a beautiful baroque facade; it contains a richly-endowed library of over 230,000 volumes. The next building on is the **Palazzo della Sapienza,** until 1935 the seat of the Roman University, with its beautiful internal courtyard, above which rises the **Chapel of Sant'Ivo della Sapienza,** by Borromini, characterised by a distinctive spiral dome.

Chapel of Sant'Ivo della Sapienza, an original work by Borromini.

The Piazza Navona

From the Corso del Rinascimento we enter Piazza Navona. Situated on the site, and retaining the shape, of the ancient Stadium of Domitian, it represents one of the most popular and most characteristic centres of the city. The piazza is adorned with three fountains, of which the central one is the famous **Fountain of the Rivers.** Commissioned by Pope Innocent X as a setting for the obelisk that rises at its centre, it was sculpted by Bernini and some of his pupils in 1650-51. The four statues placed round the grotto at the foot of the obelisk represent four rivers: the Ganges, symbolising Asia, the Nile (Africa), the Danube (Europe) and the Plate (America). At the southern end of the Piazza Navona is the **Fountain of the Moor** originally designed by Della Porta, but later modified by Bernini and G. Mari.

At the other end of the piazza is the **Fountain of Neptune.** Originally designed by Della Porta and partially realized by Bernini, this fountain long remained incomplete and it was not till 1878 that A. Della Bitta concluded the work by adding the statue of Neptune. Facing onto the Fountain of the Rivers is the **church of Sant'Agnese in Agone** (17th century), a masterpiece of baroque architecture by Rainaldi and Borromini, who designed its facade and dome.

The piazza is completed by a further three buildings: the **church of Santa Maria dell'Anima** (built in the 16th century; the baroque facade is the work of P. da Cortona of 1656), the **Chiesa di Santa Maria della Pace** (15th century) and the **Palazzo Pamphilj**. The latter, built by Rainaldi in 1650, is now the Brazilian Embassy, and contains a large hall with frescoes by P. da Cortona.

From the Ara Pacis to the Church of the Gesù, to Corso Vittorio Emanuele II

From here we reach the Piazza di Tor Sanguigna, and after a while come to the **Palazzo del Governo Vecchio,** erected in the 15th century; the **Palazzo del Banco di Santo Spirito,** designed by Sangallo and lastly the **church of San Salvatore in Lauro,** situated in the piazza of the same name. Returning in the direction from which we came, we can visit the **church of Sant'Apollinare** and the **church of Sant'Agostino.** The latter, built in the 15th century by G. da Pietrasanta using blocks of travertine spoliated from the Colosseum, has an elegant facade in the Renaissance style and is topped by the first dome to be built in the city since Roman times. Some notable works of art are preserved in its interior, such as Sansovino's statue of the *Madonna del Parto*; Raphael's fresco of *Isaiah*; Caravaggio's altarpiece of *The Madonna of the Pilgrims*; and Guercino's *Saints Augustine, John and Jerome*. Worth visiting nearby is the **Palazzo Primoli** (Via Zanardelli) which now houses the **Napoleonic Museum** containing a rich collection of objects belonging to the Bonaparte family. On the Via dei Portoghesi not far away is the **church of Sant'Antonio dei Portoghesi,** built in the early years of the 15th century but re-

modelled in the baroque style by Martino Longhi in the 17th. It contains Vanvitelli's beautiful ***Altar of the Concession***.

In a side-street (Via San Clementino) of the Via della Scrofa stands the huge **Palazzo Borghese,** built for Cardinal Dezza in 1590 and subsequently transformed by Flaminio Ponzio. The palace is entered through a large and majestic portal, which leads into the magnificent courtyard, with a garden ornamented with antiquities and fountains at its further end. We now reach the Via di Ripetta on which are situated the **churches of San Girolamo degli Illirici** (16th century) and **San Rocco,** erected in 1499 and with a handsome facade by Valadier. Adjacent to the latter is the **Mausoleum of Augustus,** built by Augustus himself in 28 B.C. as a tomb for his family. Following centuries of abandonment, it was finally restored to its original appearance in 1936. Opposite it is one of the most important Roman monuments in the city: the **Ara Pacis Augustae,** erected between 13 and 9 B.C. to celebrate the peace established by Augustus throughout the Roman world. Further on, on the Via di Ripetta, is the **Institute of Fine Arts,** Rome's main art school built by Camprese in the 19th century.

We now visit the **church of the Gesù,** which we can reach from the Piazza Venezia by taking the Via del Plebiscito until we come to the Piazza del Gesù on which the church stands. Begun by Vignola in the mid-16th century, it presents a wide and handsome facade by Giacomo Della Porta. The Gesù, mother church of the Jesuits, has a beautiful interior sumptuously decorated with frescoes, stuccoes, bronzes and polychrome marbles; again, the basic design is by Vignola. Particularly important and very spectacular is the fresco of the vault over the nave, representing the *Triumph of the Name of Jesus*, by Baciccia (Giovan Battista Gaulli), who was also responsible for the frescoes in the dome and chancel. In the left transept is the *Chapel of St. Ignatius of Loyola*, the richly. decorated monument to the founder of the Jesuits, a late-17th century work by Andrea Pozzo.

From the Gesù we continue along the **Corso Vittorio Emanuele II,** the wide thoroughfare which has swept through the city since 1881, and so arrive in the **Largo Argentina,** the large square in which have been excavated the remains of the **Area Sacra,** at one time the centre of the Campus Martius. The archaeological excavations which explored the site

Left-hand page: *Piazza Navona*.

Ara Pacis: erected to celebrate the "Augustan peace", and one of the most important Roman monuments.

in the early years of the century revealed one of the most interesting monumental complexes of Republican Rome, consisting of four temples, one of which is circular; their identification is uncertain.

Further ahead, on the Corso Vittorio, is the **Piazza di Sant'Andrea della Valle,** dominated by the **church** of the same name. Begun in the late 16th century by Grimaldi and Giacomo Della Porta, it was later completed by Carlo Maderno, who also designed the large 17th century dome. In the mid-17th century Carlo Rainaldi made alterations to the building, and gave it a sumptuous and imposing appearance especially by the addition of the facade. The church contains the tombs of the Piccolomini Popes (Pius II and Pius III), transferred here from St. Peter's, and also magnificent *frescoes* by Domenichino. Continuing along the Corso Vittorio, we see to the right the **Palazzo Massimo alle Colonne,** built by Peruzzi in c. 1530; the building presents a curving rusticated facade pierced by elegant windows. Its courtyard, embellished with ancient statues and other antiquities, is of some interest. Just after it is the **church of San Pantaleo** on the piazza of the same name, erected in 1216 but reconstructed at a later period. To one side of the piazza stands the **Palazzo Braschi,** the seat of the **Museum of Rome** since 1952; it contains interesting collections of art relating to the history of the city from medieval to modern times. The third floor of the building houses the **Contemporary Gallery of Modern Art,** in which a rich collection of works by Roman artists of the 19th century is displayed. Crossing over to the other side of the Corso Vittorio we see the **Palazzetto della Piccola Farnesina,** an elegant 16th century town house which now houses the **Barracco Museum** (ancient sculptures), the donation of Baron G. Barracco. It is followed by the **Palazzo della Cancelleria,** built in the Renaissance style, according to some, by Bramante, who was probably the architect of the magnificent courtyard. Adjacent is the **church of San Lorenzo in Damaso**; a church with very ancient origins, it was restored by Valadier in the early 19th century. From the piazza in front of the church we can enter the **Campo de' Fiori,** a piazza notorious for the sentences of death that were carried out in it and that drew crowds of spectators. Today it is the site of a lively and picturesque fruit and vegetable market.

At the centre of the piazza stands the **bronze monument to Giordano Bruno,** the well-known philosopher who was burnt here as a heretic in 1600. Turning into the Via della Corda, we now reach the harmonious **Piazza Farnese,** decorated by two twin fountains by Rainaldi. The 16th century **Palazzo Farnese**, begun by A. Sangallo, continued by Michelangelo and completed by G. Della Porta, has a majestic facade topped by a magnificent cornice decorated with Farnese lilies by Michelangelo. Inside, we make our way through A. Sangallo's magnificent **atrium**, to the **Courtyard** containing two *sarcophagi* from the Baths of Caracalla and the Tomb of Cecilia Metella. On the first floor is the **Gallery** frescoed by A. Carracci assisted by his brother and by Domenichino. The sumptuous **Salon**, occupying two floors

of the palace, is decorated with a handsome coffered ceiling and tapestry reproductions of Raphaelesque frescoes; also of interest are Della Porta's two sculptures of *Peace* and *Abundance*. In the **Sala dei Fasti Farnesiani** are some interesting frescoes by F. Salviati and T. Zuccari. Nearby is the **Palazzo Spada**, erected by G. Merisi da Caravaggio in 1540, but later transformed by Borromini. It houses the **Galleria Spada** containing distinguished works of art of the 17th century, worthy of note among which are: *Portrait of Cardinal Spada* by **G. Reni;** *Portrait of a Musician* by **Titian;** *The Apothecary* by **B. Passarotti**, as well as numerous other works by distinguished artists. We now make our way back to the Corso Vittorio Emanuele, and come to the **Chiesa Nuova** built, from 1575, over the preexisting church of San

Giovanni (12th century), after a design by M. Longhi.
The central portal is surmounted by a sumptuous loggia and various statues. The interior contains, among others, works by Barocci, Algardi and Rubens. Next to it stands the **Oratory of St. Philip Neri,** erected by Borromini in 1640.
At the end of the Corso Vittorio, the Lungotevere dei Fiorentini leads to the Principe Amedeo di Savoia Aosta bridge, close to which rises the eighteenth century dome, designed by Maderno, with its distinctive elliptical shape, of the **church of San Giovanni dei Fiorentini** (16th century). In neighbouring Via Giulia, are the 16th century **Palazzo Donarelli** and **Palazzo Sacchetti.** Further along (Via Sant'Eligio) is the **church of Sant'Eligio degli Orefici**, built in 1516 and designed by Raphael.

Left-hand page above: the Area Sacra.
Below: the characteristic square known as Campo de' Fiori.

Palazzo Farnese: a monumental sixteenth century building in whose construction A. Sangallo, Michelangelo and Della Porta all had a hand.

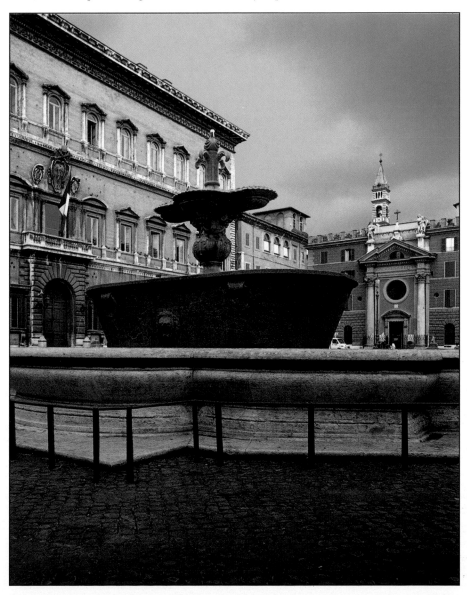

Trastevere

Again departing from Piazza Venezia, we take the Corso Vittorio Emanuele to the Largo Argentina, and from here turn left into the Via Arenula which leads to the Ponte Garibaldi over the Tiber. On the other side of the bridge we enter the characteristic district of **Trastevere.** This picturesque quarter of Rome still keeps alive its own popular traditions, and even its own dialect, which help to give it a lively and colourful atmosphere and make it the stimulating centre of local bohemian life.

From the bridge we enter the **Piazza Gioacchino Belli** with its statue of the famous poet of the same name, the author of many sonnets in the Roman dialect. It is followed by the Piazza Sonnino with the **Torre degli Anguillara,** one of the few surviving medieval towers (13th century). At the beginning of the Viale Trastevere is the **church of San Crisogono,** dating back to the 5th century but successively remodelled; the Romanesque bell-tower and the apse are in fact later (12th century). The facade is preceded by a 17th century portico, and the interior contains *frescoes* by Guercino and a *mosaic* attributed to pupils of Cavallini.

We now turn into the Via dei Genovesi on which the **church of San Giovanni dei Genovesi** is situated; founded in the 15th century, it was reconstructed in 1864. To its left is the **Hospice of the Genovesi** with a 15th century cloister considered one of the finest of the period.

In the nearby **Piazza di Santa Cecilia** stands the **church** of the same name, of ancient origins, but radically altered in the 18th century, including the addition of its *late-baroque facade* by Ferdinando Fuga; it is flanked by a Romanesque bell-tower. The interior contains a *monument* by Mino da Fiesole, a 13th century *ciborium* by Arnolfo di Cambio, and a fine *statue of Saint Cecilia* by Maderno. In the convent annexed to the church is a valuable fresco by Pietro Cavallini depicting *The Last Judgement*. From the Via Anicia we reach the Piazza di San Francesco d'Assisi, whence we continue by the Via San Francesco a Ripa to the **Basilica of Santa Maria in Trastevere.** The church, among the first to be consecrated in Rome, was begun in the 3rd century and completed in 341-52. It was reconstructed around the 12th century; it has over

Basilica of Santa Maria in Trastevere: it was one of the first Roman churches (3rd century), modified in later years.

the centuries undergone a series of architectural alterations but these have not involved substantial changes. The Romanesque bell-tower and mosaic-decorated facade date to the 12th century; the portico in front of the facade, however, is of the 18th century (C. Fontana).

The interior, with three naves, has splendid mosaics by P. Cavallini.

Just beyond the nearby Piazza Sant'Egidio is the **church of Santa Maria della Scala** (16th century), based on a design by F. da Volterra; worth noting inside is Rainaldi's *baldacchino* over the high altar. In the Via Corsini is the **Palazzo Corsini**, dating to the 15th century, but subsequently transformed by F. Fuga in 1732-36. It houses the **National Gallery of Ancient Art,** comprising a fine collection of works by Italian artists of the 17th and 18th centuries, including: *St. Sebastian* by **Rubens**; *Rest on the Flight into Egypt* by **Van Dyck**; *Views of Venice* by **Canaletto**; *St. John the Baptist* by **Caravaggio**. The palace is also the seat of Italy's most ancient academy, founded by F. Cesi in the 17th century: the **Accademia Nazionale dei Lincei.** Facing the Palazzo Corsini is the beautiful 16th century **Villa Farnesina,** designed by B. Peruzzi. Its interior was decorated by illustrious artists, including **Raphael,** who painted the famous *Story of Psyche* (on the ceiling of the gallery) and the fresco of *Galatea* which adorns another of the rooms; **Sodoma** is present with his *Nuptials of Alexander and Roxana*; **Peruzzi** and others. The building also houses the **Gabinetto Nazionale delle Stampe:** an important collection of prints and drawings (from the 15th century on).

Continuing along the Via della Lungara, we come to the late 16th century **Palazzo Salviati.** Next, the **church of Sant'Onofrio** (15th century) with frescoes by Domenichino in the portico. Inside, in the apse, a fresco by B. Peruzzi; the church contains a *monument to Torquato Tasso*, to whom a Museum has been dedicated containing manuscripts and objects belonging to this great poet. At the end of the road is the **Porta di Santo Spirito**, designed by Sangallo. Around us rise the slopes of the **Janiculum,** a delightful hill of trees and gardens and panoramic views where historical

mementos are also preserved, such as the *monument to Giuseppe Garibaldi*, executed by E. Gallori. Also on the hill is the **Villa Doria Pamphilj**; at the centre of its huge park stands the *Casino* decorated by Algardi.

Very close to the Villa Doria Pamphilj are the **church of San Pancrazio,** built over the site of the catacombs of the same name, which may be visited by descending from the church, and the **Fountain of the Acqua Paola,** built by Maderno. Also worth a visit is the **church of San Pietro in Montorio** (situated in the piazza of the same name), erected, according to tradition, on the site where St. Peter was crucified. The church, built in the 15th century and successively restored in the course of time, contains Pomarancio's *Madonna of the Letter*, the *Flagellation of Christ* (1518) by Sebastiano del Piombo, and the Raimondi Chapel designed by Bernini. The large chapels beside the altar were decorated by Daniele da Volterra and G. Vasari. *The Transfiguration*, a masterpiece by Raphael which at one time adorned the church, has been removed to the Vatican Picture Gallery. Adjacent to the church is **Bramante's Tempietto,** built by the artist for Ferdinand of Spain between 1499 and 1502. Restored at a later date, it contains some sculptures of the school of Bernini. From here we may visit the **Villa Sciarra** (reachable by way of the Via Garibaldi and then the Via Fabrizi), a 15th century building, once the property of the noble family after whom it is named and later the residence of an American diplomat, who left it to the city. It is surrounded by lush gardens, age-old trees and charming fountains. Next door is the **Bosco Parrasio,** once the rendezvous of a group of Arcadians who used to meet here to converse.

Previous page:
Trastevere (above).
Villa Doria Pamphilj (below).

Aerial view of the Church of San Pietro in Montorio where Bramante's Tempietto stands, one of the masterpieces of 17th century art.

The Castel Sant'Angelo

Commissioned by the emperor Hadrian between 130 and 140 as the burial place for himself and members of his family. The present-day Sant'Angelo bridge, the ancient Pons Aelius, linked the mausoleum with the centre of Rome. Later turned into a fortress, for which it was used from the 5th century onwards, the **Mausoleum of Hadrian** assumed the name of **Castel Sant'Angelo,** and became a prison in which such famous characters as Giordano Bruno and Cagliostro were incarcerated. It now houses a **museum** which contains ancient strong-boxes that used to contain the church treasures brought there by the Popes for safe-keeping, frescoes and various material relating to the construction of the castle; we may also visit the papal apartments (several rooms such as the Paolina Room and the Rotonda Room are richly decorated with *Mythological scenes* and with a trompe l'oeil by Perin del Vaga) and the cells of the prisoners. Worthy of mention are the **Casa dei Mutilati** and the **Palazzo di Giustizia** situated close to the castle.

Castel Sant'Angelo: views of the monument and its model reconstruction.

Vatican City

It is an independent state whose head is the Pope, Bishop of Rome and Supreme Pontiff of the Catholic Church.

The Vatican state, which was created following the Lateran Treaty on 11 February 1929, occupies the Ager Vaticanus, on the right bank of the Tiber, the site on which the first Christians, including St. Peter himself, were martyred.

ST. PETER'S BASILICA - In the year 324, Constantine erected a sumptuous Early Christian basilica in honour of the Apostle. Subsequently enriched and embellished it underwent, after 1506, the year in which Julius II commissioned Bramante with the rebuilding work, numerous alterations, carried out by Raphael, B. Peruzzi. A. Sangallo and finally Michelangelo. The latter, basing himself on Bramante's plan, conceived a huge basilica on a Greek-cross plan, topped by a magnificent double-shelled dome. In the early years of the 17th century Maderno transformed the Greek-cross into a Latin-cross plan; he was also responsible for the existing façade. Later, Bernini laid out the elliptical colonnade which seems symbolically to embrace the splendour of St. Peter's Square.

The Via della Conciliazione leads straight to the semi-circular piazza. At its centre stands an Egyptian **Obelisk** which originally graced the Circus of Nero, flanked by two **fountains** built by Maderno and Bernini; on the far side is the flight of stairs which leads up to the Basilica.

ST. PETER'S BASILICA

The facade with a broad central portico presents a series of nine balconies, of which the central one is called the **Loggia of the Benedictions.** It is in fact from this balcony that the Pontiff imparts the «Urbi et Orbi» blessing to the numerous faithful who throng St. Peter's Square. Five entrances, flanked by marble Corinthian columns which run along the facade, lead into the **Atrium,** magnificently designed by Maderno (1608-13), decorated with splendid stuccoes. Here we find **Bernini's** *equestrian statue of the Emperor Constantine* and the statue of Charlemagne by Cornacchini (16th century). Worthy of mention is the *Navicella*, a mosaic executed by **Giotto,** situated above the central

The facade of St. Peter's Basilica in the Vatican.

entrance, which was part of the primitive Basilica. The fragment of the *Angel* which was part of it has been transferred to the Vatican Crypts.

The central door by Antonio Filarete, executed between 1440 and 1445 and showing the figures of Saints Peter and Paul, constitutes a true masterpiece of the goldsmith's art; the last door to the right is the **Porta Santa,** famous throughout the world, which the Pope opens at the beginning of Jubilee years, symbolically using a ceremonial hammer.

We now enter the Basilica. We immediately realize that we have entered the most grandiose sacred building extant: a building vast in scale, conceived to celebrate the sacrality of the Catholic Church and as such full of sacred relics and wonderful works of art in a splendid fusion of the Renaissance and Baroque.

The central nave**,** at the beginning of which are two ***holy water stoups*** supported by putti (18th century), and the ***bronze statue of St. Peter*** (13th century), gives onto a series of chapels.

Chapel of the Pietà, with its famous ***Pietà***, a sculpture executed by Michelangelo when he was 24 years old, the only one to bear his signature. This work blends the classical idea of beauty with the strong emotional impact evoked by the heartrending tenderness with which the Virgin holds the dead body of Christ in her lap.

Chapel of St. Sebastian: a mosaic representing *the Martyrdom of the Saint* by Domenichino.

Chapel of the Holy Sacrament: a magnificently decorated *ciborium* by Bernini.

Gregorian Chapel: an ornately decorated 16th century chapel by Giacomo Della Porta; the altar has a precious fresco of the *Madonna del Soccorso.*

Right transept: in the passage to the Chapel of St. Michael is Canova's *monument to Clement XIII Rezzonico,* executed between 1788 and 1792.

Chapel of St. Michael: a mosaic copy of Reni's painting of the *Saint.*

Apse: the ***Cathedra Petri***, a sumptuous baroque complex created by Bernini as a setting to enclose the ancient wooden throne used, according to tradition, by Saint Peter; either side of the apse are two papal *tombs:* Bernini's *monument to the Barberini Pope Urban VIII,* and G. Della Porta's *monument to Paul III.* Let us now look upwards and admire Michelangelo's gigantic **dome,** considered the largest masonry construction of its kind. The dome, some 120 m. high, is supported by four mighty piers, in the faces of which Bernini hewed out four niches containing the colossal *statues of St. Helena, St. Veronica, St. Longinus and St. Andrew.* At the centre-point below the dome is Bernini's **Baldacchino,** the magnificent bronze canopy over the shrine of the Apostle made, according to the legend, from the bronze stripped from the pronaos of the Pantheon.

To the left of the apse is the **Chapel of the Column:** it contains Algardi's mar-

St. Peter's Basilica in the Vatican: the magnificent and monumental interior.

On the following pages: *Michelangelo's Pietà and Bernini's Baldacchino.*

ble altarpiece of *The Meeting between Leo the Great and Attila* and the tomb of the Pope. Before entering the left transept we pass the *tomb of Pope Alexander VII,* sculpted by Bernini and some of his pupils.

In the **left transept** are three altars decorated with wonderful mosaic copies of paintings, representing: *St. Joseph, Doubting Thomas* and the *Crucifixion of St. Peter.*

In the passage we see, over the entrance to the sacristy, the *monument to Pius VIII,* and then enter the **Clementine Chapel,** completed by Giacomo Della Porta and containing the *tomb of Pius VII* by Thorvaldsen.

We now enter the **left aisle:** in the passage to the right is the *monument of Leo XI* by Algardi. It is followed by the **Chapel of the Choir,** decorated with beautiful 16th century stuccoes. Just past it, to the left, is the bronze *tomb of Pope Innocent VIII* by Pollaiolo (transferred here from the old basilica). Next is the **Chapel of the Presentation** and, in the passage to the Baptistery, the *monument to the last Stuarts* by Canova. At the foot of the left aisle is the **Baptistery:** the Font consists of the cover of an ancient porphyry sarcophagus.

We can now visit the Sacristy, erected by Marchionni in 1776-84. It provides access to the **Treasury of St. Peter,** consisting of precious liturgical objects and donations made by the faithful over the centuries. Among the most striking exhibits are a 4th century sarcophagus, the magnificent ***Crux Vaticana*** richly studded with precious gems (6th century) and Pollaiolo's bronze *monument of the Della Rovere Pope Sixtus IV* (15th century). Below the Basilica are the Vatican Crypts (**Grotte Vaticane**) which contain a collection of Early Christian sarcophagi and numerous tombs of Popes. The entrance to the Crypts is under the crossing.

St. Peter's Basilica: the Tomb of Pope John XXIII (photo above) *and the tomb which tradition has it is that of St. Peter.*

THE VATICAN PALACES

The fascinating group of buildings we are about to describe has claims to be considered the most important architectural complex extant, both from the artistic and historical viewpoint. The **Vatican Palaces**, the official entrance to which is through the **Bronze Portal** to the right of St. Peter's, have undergone numerous alterations, enlargements and embellishments in the course of the centuries, and some of the most famous artists of all time have contributed to them, including Michelangelo, Bramante, Raphael and Bernini. The latter designed the majestic **Scala Regia**, the grand ceremonial staircase which leads up to the **Sala Regia** (audience hall) and the **Pauline Chapel**, decorated with beautiful frescoes by Michelangelo. The **Pontifical Apostolic Palace** is only visitable on the occasion of audiences with the Pope, who currently resides in the building added to the complex by Sixtus V. His official apartment, in which he carries out his main engagements, is on its second floor, and is preceded by the richly decorated **Clementine Hall**, to which access is given by the Papal Stairway.

Above:
Pauline Chapel.

Below: *Vatican Palaces (detail).*

The Sistine Chapel

Designed by the architect Giovannino de' Dolci for Pope Sixtus IV, it represents one of the most important complexes both from an artistic and a religious and historical point of view. It consists of a large rectangular hall, surmounted by a richly frescoed barrel vault. The **Sistine Chapel** is still the venue of important church ceremonies, notably the **Conclave**.

This traditional meeting of the Cardinals is aimed at electing the new Pope and communicating the outcome to the faithful by means of a smoke signal, black smoke indicating the inconclusiveness of the vote and the continuation of the meeting, white smoke announcing the new nomination.

The frescoes of the walls of the Sistine Chapel date to 1481-83; those of the ceiling to a quarter of a century later.

The painters involved in this sublime work of pictorial decoration include the most authoritative names in the whole world of Italian painting: first and foremost **Michelangelo**, then **Pinturicchio** and **Signorelli** and the most noted representatives of the Florentine school, such as **Botticelli**, **Ghirlandaio** and **Cosimo Rosselli**.

Let us now take a closer look at the frescoes, starting from the altar and continuing along the wall to the left:

1st painting: *The circumcision of Moses* and *The sojourn of Moses in Egypt*, by **Pinturicchio** and **Perugino**.

2nd painting: *Moses driving away the Midianites from the well, the killing of the Egyptian and the daughters of Jethro*, by **Botticelli**.

3rd painting: *Passage of the Red Sea*, by **Cosimo Rosselli**.

4th painting: *Moses receiving the tables of the Law on Mount Sinai and the adoration of the Golden Calf*, by **Cosimo Rosselli**.

5th painting: *Punishment of Korah, Dathan and Abiram*, an illustrious example of the art of **Botticelli**.

6th painting: *The reading of Moses' testament and the handing over of the rod, symbol of authority, to his successor*, a masterpiece of the art of **Luca Signorelli**.

The other series of frescoes depicts some episodes from the earthly life of Jesus.

Again starting out from the altar, we see:

1st painting: *The baptism of Christ*, by **Pinturicchio** and **Perugino.**

2nd painting: *The temptations of Jesus and the purification of the leper*, by **Botticelli.**

3rd painting: *The calling of Saints Peter and Andrew*, by **Ghirlandaio**.

4th painting: *The sermon on the mount and the healing of the leper*, by **Cosimo Rosselli**.

5th painting: *The handing over of the keys to St. Peter*, a masterpiece by **Perugino**.

6th painting: *The Last Supper*, by **Cosimo Rosselli.**

The ceiling vault was commissioned by Pope Julius II from Michelangelo, who completed the work in the space of three years (1508-1512).

This work of incomparable grandeur, though consisting of various scenes, is incredibly unified and homogeneous in effect: the Biblical stories are enclosed within a marble structure which features pairs of *Ignudi* surrounded by thrones on which alternate the huge and majestic figures of 7 *Prophets* and 5 *Sibyls*, given that the latter, in the pagan world, also predicted the coming of a different era characterized by another way of understanding man and life proper to Christianity.

In the lunettes of the windows are depicted the *forefathers of Christ* from Abraham to Joseph awaiting his birth. The central part of the ceiling represents *scenes from Genesis,* starting from above the Prophet Jonah:

- *The Creation of Light*
- *The Creation of the Stars and of Plants*
- *God the Father circling in the infinite, separating the land from the water*
- *The Creation of Adam*
- *The Creation of Eve*
- *The Fall and Expulsion from Paradise*
- *The Sacrifice of Noah*
- *The Flood*
- *The Drunkenness of Noah*

Two spandrels of the vault to the side of the Prophet Jonah are frescoed with *The Brazen Serpent* and *The Punishment of Haman*, while the corresponding spandrels on the opposite side of the ceiling, separated by the Prophet Zachariah, represent *Judith and Holofernes* and *David and Goliath*.

The end wall of the Chapel, between the two series of lateral frescoes, is the wonderful wall behind the altar painted by Michelangelo with ***The Last Judgement***.

Begun in July 1536, it was painted by the master after the decoration of the rest of the chapel had been completed.

The scene describes with dramatic crescendo and great sense of movement the turmoil, the agitation, the mood of heightened expectation of all the figures surrounding Christ, at the centre, severe and implacable in his role as Judge.

Below to the right we see the figures of the sinners massed together in the boat guided by Charon who is leading them to the underworld.

Above him, cloud-borne angels sound the trumpets of judgement.

At the feet of Christ are Saints Laurence and Bartholomew, the latter bearing the emblems of his martyrdom, the knife and flayed skin, whose face is that of the artist himself. Particularly delicate is the figure of the Virgin Mary at Christ's side.

Sistine Chapel: The Last Judgement.

Ceiling of the Sistine Chapel: detail of the "Creation of man".

The ceiling vault of the Sistine Chapel (Michelangelo). The Prophet Ezechiel.

Pages 108-110: *General view.*

Pages 111-112: *The Fall and the expulsion from Paradise.*

THE VATICAN MUSEUMS

Entered from the Viale del Vaticano, the various sectors of the Museum are reached by ascending the impressive Spiral Staircase. From here the Museums of Antiquities are situated to our left, the Picture Gallery (Pinacoteca) straight ahead, and the Museo Gregoriano Profano and Museo Pio Cristiano to our right.

THE VATICAN PICTURE GALLERY

Arranged in its present building by Pius XI, the Vatican Picture Gallery (the Pinacoteca Vaticana) consists of 15 rooms in which important paintings stretching from the primitives to the 18th century are displayed:

Room 1. The Primitives: *The Last Judgement*, a work of the 11th century by the masters Giovanni and Niccolò;

Room 2. School of Giotto and Late Gothic Masters: the room is dominated by the *Stefaneschi Triptych*, by pupils of Giotto;

Room 3. Fra Angelico, Filippo Lippi and Benozzo Gozzoli: Fra Angelico is represented by *Episodes from the Life of St. Nicholas* and the *Madonna and Child between Saints*;

Room 4. Melozzo da Forlì: *Sixtus IV appointing Platina Prefect of the Vatican Library* and *Music-making Angels*, fragments of a lost fresco by Melozzo;

Room 5. Lesser Masters of the 15th century: *The Miracles of St. Vincent Ferrer* and *Pietà* (Lucas Cranach);

Room 6. Polyptychs: especially noteworthy is a work by Crivelli: *Madonna and Child* (1482);

Room 7. Umbrian paintings of the 15th century: they include works by Perugino and Pinturicchio;

Room 8. Raphael: *Coronation of the Virgin* which the artist painted at the age of twenty; it undoubtedly represents one of the most significant works of this great painter, who was a pupil of Perugino;

Room 9. Leonardo da Vinci: *St. Jerome*, an unfinished work;

Room 10. Titian: *Madonna of St. Niccolò dei Frari*. This is followed by **Room 11**, with works by 16th century artists; **Room 12** or Baroque Room, dedicated to the painters of the 17th century with the famous *Deposition* by Caravaggio; **Rooms 13 and 14**, in

The Vatican Picture Gallery.
Above: *The Transfiguration, a work by Raphael.*
Below: *Music-making Angels: Melozzo da Forlì.*

which works of the 17th and 18th century are displayed; and lastly Room 15 or Room of the Portraits. On leaving the Picture Gallery we come (on the left) to the **Museo Gregoriano Profano:** transferred from the Lateran to the Vatican by John XXIII in recent times, it comprises *Roman sculptures* from the 1st to the 3rd century A.D. **Museo Pio Cristiano**: founded by Pius IX in the 19th century, it comprises numerous Christian artefacts found in the Catacombs and in ancient churches. **Ethnological Missionary Museum**: inaugurated in 1927, it comprises material relating to non-European cultures donated to the Museum both by numerous bequests made by the Missions and by the Missionary Exhibition (1925).

THE MUSEUMS OF ANTIQUITIES

They contain the richest collection of classical art in the world. The collection is due to the interest taken by various Popes, such as Clement XIV, Pius VI, Pius VII and Gregory XVI, who reorganized and enlarged the collection already amassed during the Renaissance. **Gregorian Egyptian Museum** - Founded by Gregory XVI, it contains sarcophagi, mummies, grave goods and other artefacts relating to the civilization of ancient Egypt. A section regarding Assyrian art has been added to it.

Pio Clementine Museum - Among the works housed in the museum, worthy of note are: the *Apollo Belvedere*, a bronze sculpture of the 4th century; the **Laocoon,** a marble group copied from a Hellenistic bronze found in 1506, which served as a model for Michelangelo and for the Mannerist movement; *Hermes*, a copy of the original by Praxiteles.

Chiaramonti Museum - In the long gallery in which it is housed are displayed a large number of sculptures; the Museum has two further sections: the **Galleria Lapidaria** and the **Braccio Nuovo**, containing the famous statue of *Augustus of Prima Porta*, one of the most celebrated portraits of the emperor, originating from the House of Livia; the **Doryphorus** by Polycleitus and a remarkable Roman work depicting the Nile. We now return to the Vestibule of the Museums of Sculpture to visit the **Hall of the Chariot**, so-called because of the presence at its centre of a Roman *chariot* of the 1st century B.C.; the room also contains the **Discobolos** by Myron, a statue of Dionysus and some sarcophagi of children.

The **Gallery of the Candelabra** consists of six sections in which are displayed copies of ancient candelabra, as well as sarcophagi, statues and fragments of precious frescoes.

Gregorian Etruscan Museum - It too founded by Pope Gregory XVI, it consists of nine rooms in which interesting archaeological material is displayed, recovered from various Etruscan cemetery sites: sarcophagi, bronzes, cinerary urns, terracottas and valuable collections of gold jewellery. We return to the Gallery of the Candelabra, through which we reach the **Gallery of the Tapestries** in which are hung ten wonderful *tapestries* of the "New School", based on designs by pupils of Raphael.

It is followed by the **Gallery of the Geographical Maps**, a corridor over 100 metres long, adorned with painted maps of Italy and her regions. We may then admire the **Gallery of St. Pius V**, consisting of two rooms containing medieval fabrics and the gallery proper in which some beautiful tapestries are displayed.

Vatican Museums: Laocoon: a wonderful marble group, a Roman copy of an original Greek bronze.

Following page: *the Belvedere torso; Discobolos by Myron; Roman chariot of the 1st century B.C.*

Above: *Gallery of the Geographic Maps: the ceiling vault.*

Below: *Lesina and Varano.*

The Stanze of Raphael

The suite of rooms known as the Stanze was frescoed by the artist on the commission of Pope Julius II, who wanted to transfer his residence from the Borgia Apartment to the second floor of the Papal Palace. The work was begun by Raphael Sanzio, then only 25 years old, in the autumn of 1508. The Pope was so struck by the genius and inspiration of the young artist that he gave him sole charge of the work, removing the commission he had previously entrusted to other distinguished artists, such as Signorelli, Pinturicchio, Perugino and Sodoma. We now enter the first of the four rooms that make up the Stanze: this is the **Room of the «*Fire in the Borgo* ».** It is decorated with the famous fresco from which it takes its name, situated on the wall facing the window. It depicts the fire which broke out in the Borgo - the district adjacent to the Vatican - in the year 847, and which was miraculously quenched by Leo IV by the sign of the cross. The second room is the so-called **Sala della Segnatura:** it was the first to be frescoed with themes relating to the four principles of human knowledge: Theology, represented by the *Disputation of the Sacrament* (or the Disputa as it is more commonly called); Philosophy with the *School of Athens*; Poetry with the *Parnassus*; and Justice with the figure of a woman, severe in aspect, accompanied by the inscription «Ius suum unicuique tribuit». The third of the rooms is the **Room of Heliodorus:** it derives its name from the large fresco situated on the wall facing the entrance and depicting *The Expulsion of Heliodorus from the Temple*. The room also contains frescoes of *Leo I stopping the Invasion of Attila*, *The Miracle of Bolsena* and *The Liberation of St. Peter from Prison*. The fourth room is the **Room of Constantine:** only completed after the death of Raphael by his pupils, it takes its name from the huge fresco of the *Battle of Constantine* which fills the long wall facing the window. After visiting the Stanze of Raphael, we can pass into the adjoining **Logge**, a long gallery in 13 bays designed by Bramante and frescoed by pupils of Raphael, based on designs he himself had produced before his premature death. The scenes portrayed are taken from the Old and New Testament. From the Room of Constantine we can also visit the **Chapel of Nicholas V,** magnificently decorated with frescoes by Fra Angelico with scenes taken from the lives of Saints Laurence and Stephen.

The Stanze of Raphael. Above: detail of the "Parnassus" (Stanza della Segnatura).

Below: the ceiling vault.

Left-hand page:
"The Fire in the Borgo"; "The School of Athens".

Detail of "The School of Athens": at the centre are depicted Plato and Aristotle, the greatest of the Greek philosophers.

Above:
*"The Expulsion
of Heliodorus
from the
Temple".*

Below:
*Room of
Constantine:
"The Baptism of
Constantine".*

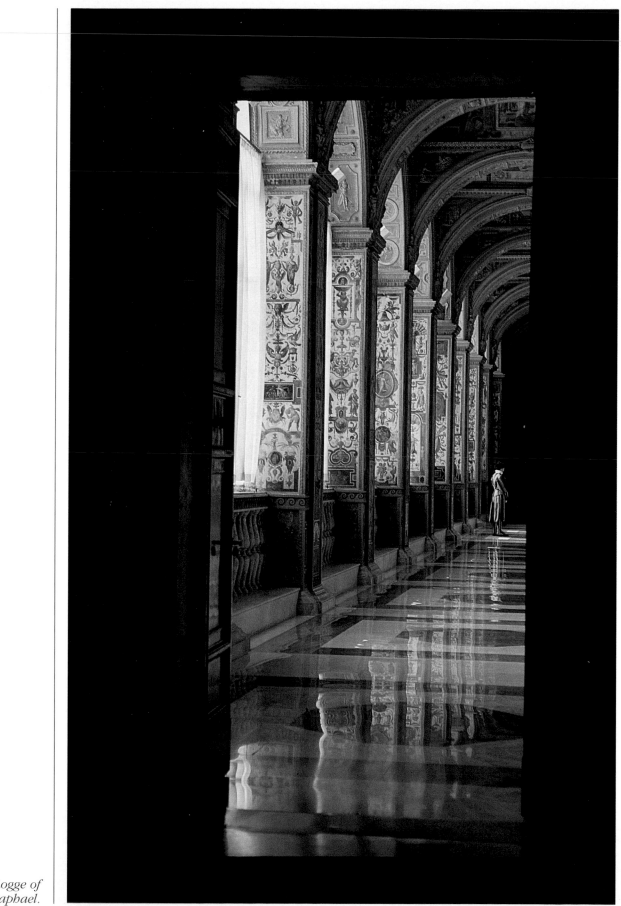

The Logge of Raphael.

THE BORGIA APARTMENT

This was the residence inside the Papal Palace of Pope Alexander VI (the Borgia Pope). He entrusted the decoration of the rooms of the apartment to the Sienese painter Pinturicchio, who completed the work together with some of his assistants in the period 1492-95. The Borgia Apartment consists of six rooms: Room 1 is the **Room of the Sibyls**: it has 12 lunettes frescoed with Sibyls and Prophets. Room 2 is the **Room of the Credo**: it derives its name from the 12 pairs of Prophets and Apostles in the lunettes, who are accompanied with verses from the Credo. Room 3 is the **Room of the Liberal Arts**: this was in fact the room used by Alexander VI as a dining-room; it was frescoed by Antonio di Viterbo with representations of the *Liberal Arts*. Room 4 is the **Room of the Saints**: almost entirely decorated by Pinturicchio, the room is notable for its beautiful frescoes, of which we may note in particular the *Disputation of St. Catherine of Alexandria before the emperor Maximian*. Room 5 is the **Room of the Mysteries**: the lunettes that decorate the room, they too by Pinturicchio, are frescoed with episodes from the life of Christ. Room 6 is the **Room of the Popes**: it is decorated with stuccoes and fantastic *grottesche* by Perin del Vaga and Giovanni da Udine. After visiting the Sistine Chapel, we can spend a little time looking at the **Collection of Modern Religious Art**. Consisting of famous paintings and sculptures only recently assembled here by Paul VI (in 1973), it is displayed in a total of 55 rooms, and includes works by **Modigliani**, **Matisse**, **Le Corbusier**, **Chagall**, **Gauguin** and others.

The Borgia Apartment - Room of the Mysteries: Adoration of the Magi, a work by Pinturicchio.

THE VATICAN LIBRARY

Founded by Pope Sixtus IV in 1475, the Vatican collection was marked by a rapid increase in the number of books it contained. Between 1587 and 1589 Sixtus V commissioned the architect **Domenico Fontana** to build a large hall, the **Sistine Hall**, to house it. It consists of two aisles divided by seven pillars and decorated with frescoes depicting scenes from the pontificate of Sixtus V. The apostolic collection contains a valuable collection of illuminated manuscripts, as well as codices and printed books.

Of the 13 rooms that compose the Vatican Library, we may mention Room I or **Museo Profano**, which houses Etruscan and Roman artefacts; **Room X**, known as the **Sala delle Nozze Aldobrandine**, in which ancient frescoes are displayed including that of the *Aldobrandine Nuptials* after which the room is named; and **Room XII** or **Chapel of Pius V**, decorated by Jacopo Zucchi.

The Vatican Library: the building was constructed in the second half of the 15th century.

Castel Gandolfo

Situated not far from Rome, this characteristic little hill-town and resort is especially famous because it is the summer residence of the Pope. The surrounding landscape is very picturesque, thanks to the presence of the charming Lake Albano - the ancient Lacus Albanus - over which Castel Gandolfo stands. At the centre of the town is the Piazza della Libertà, adorned by a *fountain* designed by Bernini. At the end of the piazza is the **Papal Palace** (17th century).

Designed by the architect Maderno, it was erected under the pontificate of Urban VIII on the site of the ancient Castle of the Savelli and later transformed. The facade is adorned with an elegant balcony (the Loggia from which the Pope gives his blessing) surmounted by a clock, and the coat of arms of Alexander VII. The interior of the palace, much changed by Pius IX, is richly decorated with stuccoes and frescoes. The ***Vatican Observatory*** annexed to it is considered one of the most important astronomical observatories in Europe. A few steps from the building we can ascend to a panoramic terrace, from where we can enjoy a wonderful view of the lake below.

One side of the piazza is delimited by the **church of San Tommaso di Villanova**, by Bernini, who also designed the fine dome by which it is surmounted. It contains some fine altarpieces by Maratta (*Assumption*); Pietro da Cortona (*St. Thomas of Villanova*); and Antonio Raggi, who was also responsible for the stuccoes that decorate the dome.

Above: *Castel Gandolfo: view of the Pope's summer residence.*
Below: *View of Lake Albano.*

Tivoli - The Villa d'Este

Tivoli lies some 30 km from Rome: it is a town of great antiquity, full of interesting reminders of its past, first and foremost the Villa d'Este. The villa, famous especially for its garden and the many fountains with which it is embellished, was built by Pirro Ligorio in 1550. The garden consists of two distinct parts joined by three large fishponds and by the Fountain of Neptune. The part of the garden on the slopes of the hill is divided by a series of paths on which a number of charming fountains are laid out, such as the Fountain of the Dragon (at the centre of the first avenue), flanked by the Fountains of Proserpine and the Organ: the Fountain of Tivoli or of the Oval, the Hundred Fountains and the Fontana del Bicchierone, to which Bernini also contributed. In the lower part of the gardens are mock-grottoes with themes of fantasy. In the centre of Tivoli it is worth visiting the **Cathedral**, an interesting baroque building begun in the 17th century but completed only much later; it is flanked by a fine Romanesque bell-tower.

On the outskirts of Tivoli stands the magnificent **Villa Adriana**, the sumptuous residence of the Emperor Hadrian, which gives the visitor an exceptional idea of Roman architecture and statuary and is one of the finest examples of an imperial residence.

Tivoli - Villa d'Este: fountains playing in the Villa gardens.

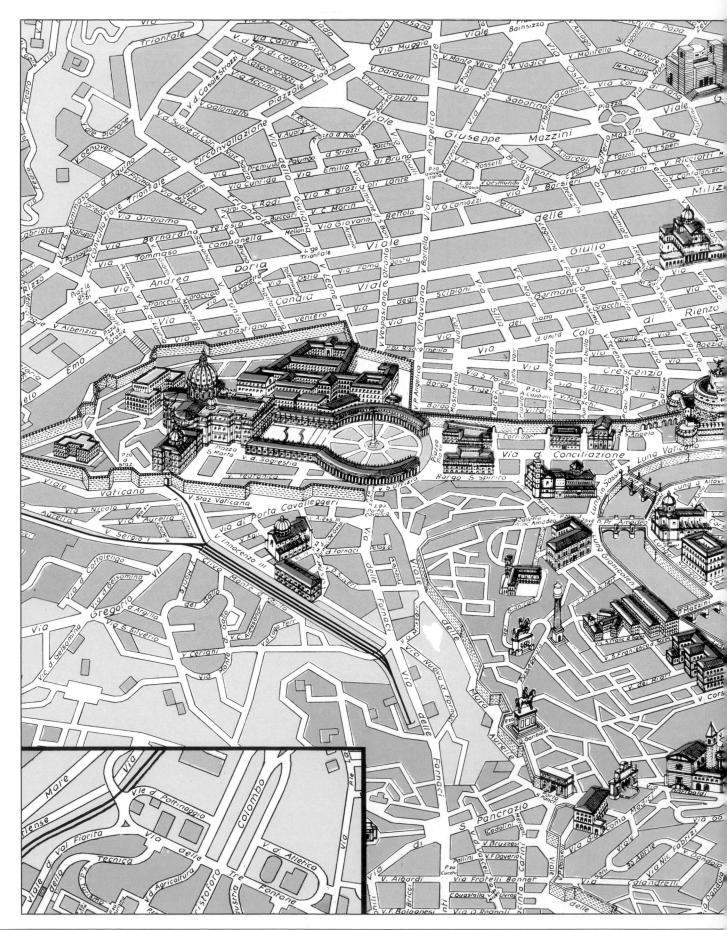